A Word to the Reader...

How often in life we suffer negative outcomes because we didn't know something important. If we don't know how dangerous wet roads can be, we may drive too fast and crash. If we don't know how identity thieves work, we may not shred important documents and end up a victim. If we don't know about computer viruses, we may not buy the correct software, and our machine could become infected.

In this book you will be introduced, maybe for the first time, to God's loving warning about future events and their impact on the inhabitants of this world. Not to know about Satan's final deceptions will be to fall for a lie and lose eternal life. The stakes could not be higher. Anyone willing to take the time to read can know for sure what is planned—what's ahead.

This well researched book from an experienced scholar is a "must read" for anyone who wants to understand current events in the light of Bible prophecy. What may seem like just another everyday occurrence could have eternal consequences.

—Thomas Mostert. President, Pacific Union Conference

Also by Herbert Edgar Douglass, Th.D.

If I Had One Sermon to Preach (editor, plus intro) – RH, 1972

Why I Joined – RH, 1973

What Ellen White Has Meant to Me (editor, plus intro) – RH, 1973

We Found This Truth – RH, 1974

Perfection: The Impossible Possibility (co-author) – SP, 1975

Why Jesus Waits – RH, 1976

Jesus—The Benchmark of Humanity (co-author) – SP, 1977

Faith, Saying Yes to God – SP, 1978

The End – PPPA, 1979

Parable of the Hurricane – PPPA, 1980

How to Survive the 80s (co-author) – PPPA, 1982

Rediscovering Joy – RH, 1994

Messenger of the Lord – PPPA, 1998

How to Survive in the 21st Century! – RH, 2000

Should We Ever Say, "I Am Saved"? – PPPA, 2003

God at Risk – AF, 2004

Feast Days – AF, 2006

They Were There – PPPA, 2006

Truth Matters – PPPA, 2006

AF = Amazing Facts
RH = Review and Herald Publishing Association
SP = Southern Publishing Association
PPPA = Pacific Press Publishing Association

Never Been This Late Before

HERBERT EDGAR DOUGLASS

Roseville, CA 95678-7275
www.amazingfacts.org

Editing by Anthony Lester
Design and page composition by Ken McFarland
Cover by Haley Trimmer

Author assumes responsibility for the accuracy of quoted
material.

ISBN: 1-58019-213-0
06 07 08 09 10 • 5 4 3 2 1

Dedication

To Norma, my God-fearing soulmate,

And to our children

Janelle, Herb, III; Mavis, Reatha, Randy,
Vivienne Sue, Donna, Chip, Judy

With whom we will march into the Kingdom together.

"NEVER BEEN THIS LATE BEFORE
is a book right on time."

—Doug Batchelor, President/Speaker, Amazing Facts

Contents

"But what matter, " said Charmides, "from whom I heard this?"
"No matter at all," I [Socrates] replied: "for the point is not
who said the words, but whether they are true or not."
—*The Dialogues of Plato*, Jewett, vol. 1, 11 (161).

Introduction

You might have heard of a young teenager in upstate Vermont whose daily job it was to clean up a clock store and adjust all the timepieces as necessary. Have you ever been in a home with several clocks that chime? How often do they all gong at once? Rarely! Trying to synchronize dozens of clocks would test anyone's endurance. But our young man was used to all the variations and performed his duties well.

However, one noontime it was different in that Vermont clock store. The teenager had done his job well—but one clock chimed 12, then 13, 14, 15, 16, 17 ... 33, 34. Well, that was too much for him. He ran from the building, shouting in the street: "It's never been this late before!"

When I read my newspaper or watch the news, I know how that teenager felt: "It has never been this late before!" If you haven't come to that conclusion, you haven't been reading newspapers— or the Bible!

Those of us over 30 have a very strong sense that someone has pushed the fast-forward button. We don't seem to be walking into the future anymore. The future seems to be galloping into us! In fact, we can hardly get our breath before the next news program reminds us—"It's never been this late before!"

This is no time for half-hearted repentance, no time for a permissive gospel that promises a Savior from the penalty of sin but no Savior from the power of sin. This is no time for "soft gospel-lite" that doesn't produce overcomers!

This is no time for confusing confession for repentance, or for casual witnessing for Christ, or for playing church! Too many dress up for weddings but dress down for church! Too many are making the Sabbath into a holiday, but not God's holy day! Too many think that they can be closer to God on a mountaintop or at the beach than in church! Dangerous thinking! Too many have been taking spiritual holidays—it's time to come back to reality. We are living in the end of the time of the end! "It's never been this late before!"

Events foretold in the Bible are now being fulfilled that were not even on the horizon 25 years ago! Yes, we talked about some of them, in a general way, something like a guessing game, but none of us then could point to events even remotely like what we see on the television today.

In these pages we shall look at some of these predictions that we have merely romanticized about for years. "It's never been this late before!" We will trace carefully the rise of world esteem for the papacy, the exponential rise of natural calamities, the tsunami of New Spirituality that has swept over most Evangelical churches, including some of our own. We will note how major nations are becoming of "one mind," not only politically but also economically. We will observe how the world generally is facing the worst of economic collapses.

We will also examine the remarkable attention that people everywhere are giving to psychic phenomena. And we will scrutinize how satanic methods, successful since Eden, such as pretence, scapegoating, confusion, and coercion, are reaching their zenith in capturing the minds of young and old. "It has never been this late before!"

What can we do about all this? Our first responsibility is to be alert to reality. None of these issues will "go away." They will only become more visible, more front and center. No one will escape, no matter how often they turn off their TVs or radios or cancel newspapers and weekly news magazines.

Our second responsibility is to eagerly seek the promise of Jesus—that He will "never leave you nor forsake you" (Hebrews 13:5). No matter how crushing future plans might turn out, no matter how terrifying circumstances may become, we will have the quiet confidence of knowing that we were not caught by surprise—"these things I have told you, that when the time comes, you may remember that I told you of them" (John 16:4).

What a time to be alive! "It is later than you think."

Herbert Edgar Douglass
Lincoln, California
June, 2006

♦ CHAPTER ONE ♦

Tsunami of Disasters—What's New?

Y ou're right! We have always had terrific disasters, whether natural or manmade! Religious leaders since the second century have looked at the world around them and declared that they were indeed living in the "last days."

With one eye on Matthew 24 and the other on local and world news, Cyprian (ca. 200–258), Bishop of Carthage, wrote: "That wars continue frequently to prevail, that death and famine accumulate anxiety, that health is shattered by raging diseases, that the human race is wasted by the desolation of pestilence, know that this was foretold; that evils should be multiplied in the last times, and that misfortunes should be varied; and that as the day of judgment is now drawing nigh, the censure of an indignant God should be more and more aroused for the scourging of the human race" (Treatise V, par. 5, in *Ante-Nicene Fathers* (ANF), vol. 5, 459).

Pope Gregory the Great (ca. 540–604) wrote: "And now that the end of the world is approaching, many things are at hand which previously have not been; to wit, changes of the air, terrors from heaven, and seasons contrary to the accustomed order to times, war, famine, pestilences, earthquakes in divers places." (*Post-Nicene Father PNF*), bk. 11, ep. 66, vol. 13, 82.) But even further:

13

"Indeed among the clergy and people of this city [Rome] there has been such an invasion of feverous sicknesses that hardly any freeman, hardly any slave, remains fit for any office ministry. Moreover, from the neighbouring cities we have news daily of havocs and of mortality. Then, how Africa is being wasted by mortality and sickness I believe that you know more accurately than we do, insomuch as you are nearer to it. But of the East those who come from thence report still more grievous desolations. In the midst of all these things, therefore, since you perceive that there is a general smiting as the end of the world draws near, you ought not to be too much afflicted for your own troubles" (*PNF*, bk. 9, ep. 123, vol. 13, 27).

Many more similar quotations could be recalled. So what's new about the twenty-first century? [1]

Earthquakes

Take earthquakes, for example. One of the deadliest earthquakes in known history occurred in Aleppo, Syria, in A.D. 1138, killing more than 230,000 people. But in 1201, the deadliest earthquake of all time hit the eastern Mediterranean, killing approximately 1.1 million people. In 1556, an earthquake in Shaanxi, China, killed more than 830,000 people. To put all this in perspective, the San Francisco earthquake, April 18, 1906, killed about 700 with 2,100 added in the ensuing fire.

Of course, Cyprian and Gregory the Great were correct. Huge earthquakes with enormous loss of lives have occurred in probably every century for which we have records. But what I find interesting is the *increasing* number of first-class earthquakes since 1775 (for the sake of a date) when Portugal was rocked with the "Lisbon" earthquake, killing more than 100,000 people. (I know the argument—we just have better tools for measuring earthquakes, etc., in modern times. But that doesn't hold water compared to the death statistics alone.)

---

1. Statistics for deaths in earthquakes, famines, pestilence, hurricanes, etc., are from http://across.co.nz/WorldsWorst Disasters.html April 6, 2006, http://www.guinessworldrecords.com/content April 6, 2006, http://www.nhe.noaa.gov/pastdead.html April 7, 2006, http://en.wikipedia.org/wiki/Tsunami April 9, 2006, http://en.wikipedia.org/wiki/Death_toll April 9, 2006.

Let's take a fast overview since 1755:

Country	Year	Number of Deaths
Iran	1780	200,000+
Italy	1908	123,000+
Italy	1915	30,000+
China	1920	200,000+
Japan	1923	170,000+
China	1927	200,000+
China	1932	70,000+
Pakistan	1935	30,000+
Chile	1939	28,000+
Turkey	1939	32,000+
Turkmenistan (USSR)	1948	110,000+
India	1950	30,000+
Bangladesh	1970	500,000+
Peru	1970	66,000+
China (Tangshan)	1976	600,000+ (largest in modern times)
Guatemala	1976	30,000+
Iran	1978	28,000+
Armenia	1988	100,000+
Iran	1990	50,000+
Bangladesh	1991	139,000+
Iran	2003	26,271
South Asia	2004–2005	85,000+
Pakistan/Afghanistan	2005	50,000+

(Many modern earthquakes, such as Long Beach, CA, 1933; Chile, 1960; Alaska, 1964; Loma Prieta, CA, 1989; Turkey, 1999, etc., caused extensive damage, but loss of life was relatively minimal.)

What we have just looked at is a startling trumpet call—notice the increase of incidences. It has never been this late before! Later in this chapter, we will make further connections to these end times.

Famines and Droughts

Devastating famines are another feature of Christ's prophecy concerning the end times found in Matthew 24 and Luke 21. Christian leaders for the past 2,000 years have believed that extensive famines in their day were fulfilling these prophecies. And they too were right. However, Jesus said that famines, pestilences, earthquakes, and wars were but "the beginning of sorrows [birth pangs]—but *"the end is not yet"* (Matthew 24:8, 6).

Let's take a quick look at the facts. Obviously not every famine has been recorded since the first century A.D. And we know that super famines have occurred on all continents through the centuries before and after Christ. For instance, famine in Japan in 1181 wiped out at least 100,000 people. In India, 1769, about 10 million lost their lives in the Bengal famine. Ireland's "potato famine" in 1845–48 took at least a million lives. The deadliest drought in recorded history occurred in China between 1876 and 1879. Most crops dried up, livestock died, no food production occurred in a one million square kilometer area of nine provinces, causing the death of more than nine million people!

A few years later in north China, another drought and famine took at least 500,000 lives. Again in China, 1942–1943, a drought and ensuing famine in the Henan province killed more than a million people. And once again in China 1958–1961, 20 million died in that famine.

Now think Africa, 1981–1984—rivers and lakes dried up from drought with the incredible impact on 20 African countries. During one season, about 20,000 were starving to death each month! Combined with other relatively recent African famines, the death total is well over one million people. Probably no one has kept count of the deaths in the ongoing Somalia famine—perhaps beyond the ability for anyone to keep an accurate account.

North Korea during the last 10 years is said to have lost more than four million people from famine and floods, but who really knows how many more?

And who can forget the American Midwest during the drought of the 1930s. Many died of lung diseases and starvation. Thousands of farmers went bankrupt and 350,000 people deserted the region. Or perhaps what has been described as the greatest loss of farmland due to drought in modern times—in Portugal, where, since 1970, more than 50 percent of formerly tillable land is unusable.

Again, in this fast overview, we note the intriguing *persistency* and *increasing* horror of modern famines, at a time when we are producing more food than the world needs, but without the ability to get the food where it is needed most.

Pestilence

Pestilence is a horrid word. It is a word picture that terrorizes families everywhere today. Just think that worldwide, 2.5 million people are still dying annually from malaria! The following numbers are staggering:

Pestilence	Date	Killed
Bubonic Plague—Europe	1347–1350	25 million+
Smallpox	1775–1782	130,000+
Worldwide influenza	1918–19	35–100 million
Asian Flu	1957	400,000+
AIDS	1981-	25 million+

The pattern we have shown in earthquakes and famines continues. In the last 15 years, what appears to be a modern phenomenon has gripped the minds of medical researchers—Bovine

Spongiform Encephalopathy (BSE), commonly known as Mad Cow Disease, a variation of Creutzfeldt-Jakob disease. The most common cause is infected beef, but even vegetarians die from BSE, probably from using bone meal in their gardens.

Statistics are hard to come by. Research indicates that scientists and medical doctors have had great difficulty in going public with their findings. Because there is no way to actually test a patient to see if they have BSE before they die, physicians tend to misdiagnose BSE for Alzheimer's disease and other related diseases. Research indicates that 10 percent of Alzheimer's patients actually had BSE or CJD.[2]

"Fatal Contact: Bird Flu in America," a two-hour, major television drama on ABC was aired on May 9, 2006. Human bodies died so quickly that dump trucks hauled them away as animal carcasses and were torched to help stop the plague. Called a "thinking man's disaster film," this possible global pandemic is issued as a "wake-up" call.[3]

Hurricanes

It's not always easy to track the loss of life in severe hurricanes, but generally masters of statistics agree on the following:

Hurricane (Typhoon, Cyclone)	Date	Category	Loss of Life or Cost
India	1737	?	300,000+
South Carolina/Georgia	1881	?	700+
Louisiana	1893	?	2,000+
South Carolina/Georgia	1893	?	2,000+
Texas (Galveston)	1900	4	800+

2. Sources include Michael Balter, "Bent Out of Shape," Science, March, 2001; Robert Cohen, "Is Mad Cow Disease in America?" http://www.notmilk. come/milatoz.html. May 10, 2004; David Kidd, "What Vegetarians Need to Know About Mad Cow Disease," Vegetarian Voice, Summer, 2001 as cited in research paper, May 2004, by Kelli Douglass.

3. Associated Press, April 28, 2006, cited in http://abcnews.go.com/ Entertainment/wireStory?id

Mississippi/Alabama	1906	3	134+
Louisiana	1909	4	350+
Texas (Velasco)	1909	3	41+
Florida	1910	3	30+
Louisiana (New Orleans)	1915	4	275+
Texas (Galveston)	1915	4	275+
Louisiana	1918	3	34+
Florida (Keys)	1919	4	1,836+
Florida/Alabama	1926	4	243+
Puerto Rico	1928	4	312+
Florida (Lake Okeechobee)	1928	4	1,836+
Texas (Freeport)	1932	4	40+
Texas (South)	1933	4	40+
Florida (Keys)	1935	5	408+
New England	1938	3	600+
Northeast USA	1944	3	390+
Florida/LA/MS	1947	4	50
HAZEL (SC/NC)	1954	4	95+
CAROL	1954	3	60
DIANE (N.E. USA)	1955	1	184
AUDREY (LA/TX)	1957	4	390
DONNA (FL/Eastern USA)	1960	5	50
DONNA (St. Thomas, VI)	1960	4	225
CARLA (TX)	1961	4	46
HILDA (LA)	1964	3	38
BETSY (FL/LA)	1965	3	75
BEULAH (TX)	1967	4	?
CAMILLE (MS/LA)	1969	5	256
AGNES (N.E. USA)	1972	1	184
DAVID (Caribbean)	1979	5	?
HUGO (SC)	1989	4–5	$7 Billion
ANDREW (FL)	1992	5	30
FRAN (NC)	1996	3	$4 Billion

OPAL (FL)	1995	3	12
MITCH (Guad/Honduras)	1998	5	?
BONNIE (NC)	1998	3	?
GEORGES (Carib/FL/MS)	1998	4	$6.6 billion
VANCE Australia	1999	5	?
FLOYD (So Carolina)	1999	3	$4.5–6 billion
LILY	2002	2–4	$900 million
ISABEL	2003	5	$3.4 billion
IVAN	2004	5	124 / $15 billion
CHARLIE (Florida)	2004	4	35 / $14 billion
KATRINA (LA, MI, AL)	2005	3–5	1525 / $50 billion
RITA (TX)	2005	3–5	54
WILMA (Florida/MS)	2005	4–5	481 / $10 billion
STAN (Guatemala)	2005	1	1,500+ / $2 billion
GLENDA (Australia)	2006	4–5	?
LARRY (Australia)	2006	5	?
South China Sea	2006	Strongest typhoon on record	

On December 2, 2005, Hurricane Epsilon developed, making it the 14th of 2005, setting yet another record for the number of hurricanes in a single year.

It doesn't take even a high school graduate to figure out the pattern we have been seeing in our overview of previous natural disasters. Note the modern intensities. Ponder the *persistency* and *increased activity* and measure your own perception.

Sea and Waves Roaring

Floods have proven to be the deadliest natural disasters, mainly because population densities settle around rivers and shores. In addition, diseases prompted by the floodwaters probably kills more people than the actual floods.

I will first separate flooding disasters from floodwaters caused by typhoons, hurricanes, or cyclones.[4]

Flooding rivers

Location	Year	Number of Deaths
Yellow River, China	1887	900,000–2,000,000
Johnstown, PA	1889	2,200
Kansas City, Missouri	1903	200
Willow Creek, Oregon	1903	200
Mississippi Valley	1912	200
Ohio River, Ohio, Kentucky	1913	700
Santa Paula, CA	1928	450
Yellow River, China	1931	1,000,0000–3,700,000
Yangtze River, China	1931	145,000
Mississippi Valley	1937	1,100
Yellow River, China	1938	500,000–900,000
Rapid City, SD	1972	237
Man, WV	1972	118
Ru River, Banqiao Dam	1976	230,000
Loveland, CO	1975	139[5]

Floods caused by tsunamis, generated by volcanoes or earthquakes

Location	Year	Number of Deaths
Lisbon, Portugal	1755	90,000+
Krakatoa, Indonesia	1883	36,000+
Newfoundland, Canada	1929	28

---

4. All three describe the same natural phenomenon: Typhoons in the Pacific Ocean, Hurricanes in the Atlantic, and Cyclones in the Indian Ocean.

5. The good news of fewer river floods in the United State in recent years is due to the massive flood relief programs subsidized by federal and state funds. In China, for the past several years, an enormous dam is being built on the Yellow River to forestall future flooding.

Pacific, Aleutians, Hawaii	1946	165
Chile, Hawaii, Japan	1960	2,289
Vajont Dam, Italy	1963	2,000
Good Friday Alaska-Calif	1964	159
Moro Gulf, Philippines	1976	7,000+
Tumaco, Columbia/Ecuador	1979	300+
Western Japan	1983	104
Okushira, Japan	1993	250+
Papua New Guinea	1998	2,200+

(deadliest in recorded history)[6]

Wars and Rumors of Wars

Jesus surely had it right—anyone looking at the last 2,000 years would not find great evidence for evolutionary hope in the human race wherein every year, everything should get better and better. Although completely accurate records of deaths due to wars are not available, we can make some acceptable judgments.

Conflict	Year/Span	Number of Deaths
Russo-Japanese War	1904–1905	150,000
World War I	1914–1918	15–66 million
		(includes Spanish Flu deaths)
Mexican Revolution	1910–1920	300,000–2 million
China Warlord Period	1917–1928	200,000–800,000

6. The *Washington Post*, October 16, 2005, reported: "The international disaster-relief community is overstretched, with killer earthquakes, hurricanes and famines from New Orleans to Niger and Pakistan competing for public attention and charitable dollars, according to U.N. and private relief officials. The amount of donations for the deadly earthquake in Pakistan and flooding in Central America has come in at a slower pace than for other recent calamities, officials say. Two major disasters during the past year— Hurricane Katrina and the Indian Ocean tsunami—have sapped funding for other causes and contributed to what experts call "donor fatigue" among governments that finance the United Nations' efforts and individual givers who support private agencies. "I've never seen a year quite like this one," said Carolyn Miles, the head of operations for the relief agency Save the Children.

Russian Civil War	1917–1921	5–8 million
Finnish Civil War	1918	35,000
Chinese Civil War	1928–1949	1.3–6.1 million
		(excluding World War II)
Sino–Japanese War	1931–1945	10–25 million
Chaco War (Paraguay/Bolivia)	1932–1935	100,500
Spanish Civil War	1936–1939	360,000–1 million
World War II	1939–1945	62 million
Vietnam War	1945–1975	2.3–3.1 million
		(U.S.,'65–'75, 1.75–2.1 mill.)
Korean War	1950–1953	1.5–3.5 million
Algerian Independence	1954–1962	100,000–1 million
Guatemala Civil War	1960–1996	200,000
North Yemen Civil War	1962–1970	150,000
Biafran War (Nigeria)	1967–1970	1 million
Northern Ireland	1969–1998	3,600
First Burundi Civil War	1972	300,000
Turkish/Cyprus	1974	5,000
Ethiopian Civil War	1974–1991	230,000–1.4 million
Lebanese Civil War	1975–1990	150,000
Khmer Rouge	1975–1979	1.7–2.3 million
Angolan Civil War	1975–2002	500,000
Mozambique Civil War	1976–1993	900,000–1 million
Russian Afghanistan	1979–2001	1.5–2 million
Ugandan Civil War	1979–1986	500,000
Sino–Vietnam War	1979	30,000
Iran–Iraq War	1980–1988	1 million
El Salvador Civil War	1980–1992	75,000
Sri Lanka/Tamil	1983–	60,000
Peru/Shining Path	1980–	69,000
Falklands War	1982	1,000
Sudanese Civil War	1983–2002	1 million
Turkish/PCK Conflict	1984–	30,000
South Yemen Civil	1986	13,000

Somali Civil War	1988–	550,000
Liberian Civil War	1989–	220,000
Romanian Revolution	1989	1,500
Algerian Civil War	1991–	120,000
Gulf War	1991	100,000
First Congo War	1991–1997	800,000
Sierra Leone Civil War	1991–2000	200,000
Croatian Independence	1991–1995	12,000
Bosnia	1992–1995	278,000
First Chechen War	1994–1996	50,000–200,000
Kosovo War	1996–1999	7,000 (disputed)
Ethiopia–Eritrea War	1998–2000	75,000
Second Congo War	1998–2004	3.8 million
Second Chechen War	1999–	31,000–100,000
USA/Afghanistan War	2001–2002	20,000–49,600
Côte d'Ivoire Civil	2002–	3,000
Coalition/Iraq	2003–	36,000–120,000

If we were to include those countries currently that have *internal* conflicts, primarily over religious differences, the list would be much longer: Afghanistan, Bosnia, Côte d'Ivoire, Cyprus, East Timor, India, Indonesia, Kashmir, Kosovo, Kurdistan, Macedonia, Middle East, Nigeria, Northern Ireland, Pakistan, Philippines, Russia/Chechnya, South Africa, Sri Lanka, Sudan, Tibet, and Uganda.

As I write, day after day, pending world crises get more ominous. And these are not petty border skirmishes! On April 16, 2006, the Israeli Ambassador to the United Nations, Dan Gillerman, warned that recent statements by the Palestinian government, Iran, and Syria "are clear declarations of war." Gillerman warned that "a dark cloud is looming above our region, and it is metastasizing" and that the danger is "not just to Israel but also to the whole free world, and to civilization as we know it, as this axis of evil and terror sows the seeds of the first world war of the 21st century."[7]

---

7. Associated Press, April 17, 2006, cited in http://www.breitbart.com/news/2006/04/17/D8H25KGO1.html

What does all this mean?

What should we do with all this information covering mostly the last 100 years? Let's look again at our Lord's prophecies. In Matthew 24 and Luke 21, wars, earthquakes, hurricanes, pestilences, and floods would be "the beginning of sorrows" (Matthew 24:8). In other words, these are not, in themselves, specific signs of the end of the world.

However, Jesus did not leave us with a guessing game! God does not play hide-and-seek and He does not enjoy watching us be befuddled regarding what He has called "the end of the age [this world as we know it]." He has given us specific signs as to when His loyalists will know when His return is "near" (Matthew 24:33).

He did also specify other signs that would be perceived as something very special, such as a darkened sun at midday, a moon that would not give its usual light, and a night when there would be an astonishing star display (verse 29). He compared the last days of Planet Earth to the last days before Noah entered the ark (verses 37–39). And He gave us a clue—His return would be delayed as noted in the delay in the Bridegroom's appearance at his wedding (25:5). We will discuss that "delay" later.

"Birth pains"

Here's a specific clue that will help us. Jesus said, "All these are the beginning of sorrows" (Matthew 24:8). "Sorrows" is a translation of the Greek word for "birth pangs" or "labor pains."

Every mother and father knows exactly what Jesus was telling us. Closing in on nine months, the growing child within the womb is telling Mother that she should be preparing for his or her grand appearance. And Mother is telling Father that he should be reviewing his responsibilities—car filled with gas, crib in the bedroom, etc.

Then those predicted "labor pains!" The end is near! Perhaps 20 minutes apart. A day might go by, and then 10 minutes apart. Then five minutes. Time to get in the car. Two minutes. Time to be in the hospital!

As the "labor pains" become *closer together*, they become more *intense*. The signs were clearly understood because the parents had done their homework! Jesus has told us that His followers in the "last days" will catch the increasing tempo of events, even as a wise mother and father should.

Never Been This Late Before

In this chapter, we have reviewed the "birth pangs" of the end times. In fact, while I was eating breakfast today, the news commentator focused on the rash and rage of tornadoes through the southern United States: "We have had almost three times the tornadoes this year compared to 2005!" I call that increased "birth pangs!"

For too long, I, with most of you, have only romanticized words that Ellen White wrote: "Famines will increase. Pestilences will sweep away thousands. Dangers are all around us from the powers without and satanic workings within, but the *restraining power of God* is now being exercised" (*Last Day Events*, 27, emphasis added). We had no way of relating to these words anymore than young wives can relate to what their mothers said about "birth pangs!" But the time comes when mothers-to-be sing out, "Now I know what you mean!"

But this quotation is even more insightful: "These wonderful manifestations will be *more and more frequent and terrible* just before the second coming Christ and the end of the world, as signs of its speedy destruction" (White, *Patriarchs and Prophets*, 108, emphasis added).

"More frequent and terrible!" "Birth pangs!" Remember our chapter theme: **Jesus will return after this planet has endured an unprecedented, exponential rise of natural disasters—note "unprecedented" and "exponential"!**

The exponential curve

One closing thought—what do I mean by "exponential"? The exponential curve is shaped like a slope that constantly increases upward in contrast to a gradual upward increase of a straight line. We use this curve in many areas in the scientific world as well as the financial world. For example, think of interest on savings in your bank account. If you want to know how much $100,000 will become in 10 years at 8-percent interest, you can draw a gradual straight line up adding $8,000 the first year, $8,000 the second year, etc. In 10 years you would have $80,000 earned interest (that is, you would now own $180,000). In 30 years, you would own $215,892.

But if you were earning compound interest at 8 percent, you would not have a predicted straight line of $8,000 per year, but a line that would slope up continually and always getting *more vertical*. At the end of the second year, you would own $116,640 (not $116,000); end of third year, $125,971 (not $124,000); end of fourth year, $136, 048, (not $132,000). At 30 years, you would own $1,006,266. Compare!

Now how does this apply to last-day events? All the awful catastrophes of the past will be repeated, but in exponential rapidity. Very much like the mother's labor in childbirth! Can anyone deny that hurricanes, floods, famines, pestilences, national debt, personal debt, bankruptcies, moral degradation, depletion of water aquifers, energy consumption, civil wars, international crises, etc., are increasing with astonishing speed? Most people live with the sense that everything is out of control compared to the life we lived even 25 years ago. There seems to be no way to turn back the clock. The escalator, either down or up, seems to go faster every day with every news broadcast. And everyone has the lurking feeling that they can't get off that escalator.

The sense of escalation is heightened when the latest disaster is wired into our living rooms through CNN or FOX News in living color. Instantly, we are fed the reporter's hype and this constant feed gives us the feeling that it is happening more rapidly, that we are surrounded with distress, and that it has never happened like this before. Our perceptions are only adding to the reality around us.[8]

It has never been this late before.

---

8. I am well aware of some who declare that our "perceptions" are due to better, worldwide communications and we "feel" that everything is worse. And true, death tolls are marvelously less in modern tornadoes, hurricanes, floods, etc., because we have a remarkable improvement in early warning systems.

Theme: Jesus will return after the world has
had its worst economic collapse.

♦ CHAPTER TWO ♦

International Financial Collapse

How could all this be—an international financial collapse?
This world has so many checks and balances in a global
economy! ... Never could happen? Listen to God as He lets
us in on our future. Perhaps very soon now!

Revelation 18:11, 17—– *"And the merchants of the earth will weep
and mourn over her, for no one buys their merchandise anymore. ...
For in one hour such great riches came to nothing."* Sounds global,
and it sounds dire! No place to run. The gas tank goes dry. Nothing
is for sale! What should we make of this prediction?

I know—some are thinking, "Where has Douglass been the
last 20 years?" Life on this planet is not what it used to be. Think
of that silicon chip and how Apple Computer ballooned into a
multibillion dollar company overnight, and IBM gave the world
the PC, then Microsoft, Intel, Dell, etc. That computer chip got
cheaper, much cheaper, and we packed it into everything—car
engines, lawnmowers, pagers, and pocket phones, and laptops got
smaller. And what we have today will be looked at with nostalgia
in the next five years—that little piece of plastic with a few crossed
wires and some solder turned the world upside down, and we
haven't seen anything yet! No question about it!

Yet is there anyone who reads the newspaper or watches a TV newscast still thinking that the countries of the world are not in an unparalleled economic quandary? If I were to list what the leading politicians and economists are saying about our current financial instability, the quotations would be endless.

Bond King

For starters, listen to Bill Gross, known as the Bond King: "Let me state categorically that the following sequence is barely questionable, almost inevitable, 99 percent unavoidable, and in modern parlance, a slam dunk. What's inevitable? A recession in the next year or two. Why? 1) Housing prices fall, at least 15 percent and much more on the two coasts; 2) People will stop taking equity out of their homes, which will cause the recession. Why a recession? Because 50 percent of the jobs gained in the past three years were related to housing expansion. We are losing manufacturing jobs; outsourcing technical jobs, gaining jobs in service industries such as at Wal-Mart and Pizza Hut; pensions are going under by the billions of dollars; energy costs will skyrocket as will property taxes and medical expenses."[1]

Why do keen economists talk like this? For starters—because they see China and Japan owning more U.S. treasury bonds than Americans do and they can pull the plug at anytime. Why would they? Because they see Americans individually and as a nation *owing* far more than they own ... far more. Because they see most Americans living from pay check to pay check with no foreseeable hope of paying off their credit cards, in a land where bankruptcies are soaring—where the slightest crisis is poised to bring the whole national and international economy to a standstill and chaos.

Think about what is ahead with further increases in interest rates that will put hundreds of thousands of homeowners in jeopardy, especially those who have bought with little or no down payment or with ARMs (adjustable rate mortgages that will increase monthly with the rise of interest rates).

We all have seen within a few short weeks in 2005 how two

---

1. October 3, 2005 newsletter.

hurricanes can spin everything I have just written further out of control—energy costs, increased taxes, and sky-high concern for everyone of us who pays for it all. All this country needs to shove it into a first-class national panic would be an earthquake in Los Angeles or San Francisco. And something like that will happen. That is a given!

Perpetual Denial

But most of us live in perpetual denial—especially those who never lived during the 1929–1939 Depression. Huge food lines filled with the unemployed, who once had a secure job; many banks closed forever; huge tariffs on buying imported goods, which meant that foreign countries would not buy the dwindling production in the United States; coupled with the worst drought on American soil, which raised the cost of food and bankrupted many thousands—the picture was worse than words can describe. The only event that brought America out of the Depression was World War II. It suddenly provided jobs for our factories, and the money began to flow as the federal government *borrowed* itself into renewed prosperity.

Let no one think that the United States learned its lesson and such misery could never be repeated. Former Federal Reserve Chairman Paul Volcker said recently, "We face a 75 percent chance of a crisis within the next five years."

Richard Rubin, former Treasury Secretary warned, "We're facing a day of serious reckoning." Those who are listening expect income taxes to triple, the value of our homes to plummet, stocks on Wall Street to get chopped off at the knees, Social Security and Medicare payouts to be slashed in half, and cushy retirement pensions to be kissed goodbye.

Red Queen's Race

I am reminded of Lewis Carroll's *Through the Looking Glass*[2] and his Red Queen's Race: "The Queen kept crying 'Faster!' but

---

2. *Alice's Adventures in Wonderland & Through the Looking-Glass* (New York: New American Library, Signet Classic, 2000), 146, 147.

Alice felt she could not go faster, though she had no breath to say so. The most curious part of the thing was, that the trees and the other things round them never changed their places at all: however fast they went, they never seemed to pass anything. 'I wonder if all the things moved along with us?' thought poor puzzled Alice. And the Queen seemed to guess her thoughts, for she cried, 'Faster! Don't try to talk!'

"Not that Alice had any idea of doing that. She felt as if she would never be able to talk again, she was getting out of breath: and still the Queen cried, 'Faster! Faster!' and dragged her along. 'Are we nearly there?' Alice managed to pant out at last.

" 'Nearly there!' the Queen repeated. 'Why, we passed it 10 minutes ago! Faster!' And they ran on for a time in silence, with the wind whistling in Alice's ears, and almost blowing her hair off her head, she fancied.

" 'Now! Now!' cried the Queen. 'Faster!' Faster!' And they went so fast they seemed to skim through the air, hardly touching the ground with their feet, till suddenly, just as Alice was getting quite exhausted, they stopped, and she found herself sitting on the ground, breathless and giddy. The Queen propped her against a tree, and said kindly, 'You may rest a little now.'

"Alice looked round her in great surprise. 'Why, I do believe we've been under this tree the whole time! Everything's just as it was!"

"Of course it is,' said the Queen. 'What would you have it?'

"Well, in our county,' said Alice, still panting a little, 'you'd generally get to somewhere else—if you ran very fast for a long time, as we've been doing.'

" 'A slow sort of country!' said the Queen. 'Now, here, you see, it takes all the running you can do, to keep in the same place. If you want to get somewhere else, you must run at least twice as fast as that!' "

The moral? Most every man or woman alive feels that they must run faster just to stay even in balancing their budget. Since 2000, the U.S. economy has grown by $1.4 trillion (inflation-adjusted, gross domestic product growth—GDP). But over the same period, total credit market debt outstanding has grown by an astounding $9 trillion. Personal (household) debts alone have exploded by 60 percent over the past five years, from already elevated levels ($6.9 trillion to $11 trillion). Nearly 90 percent of the reported GDP was in consumption and residential building! On top of all this, capital spending in the United States is stuck in limbo, real wages are barely keeping up, if at all, and *private* sector employment has risen only one percent since 2000!

Somehow through the past 25 years, the United States and most other developed nations are enjoying the anesthetic of financial fantasy. People have come to believe that they can build heaven on earth, where thanks to the ever-improving miracles of central banking with its endless supply of paper money, medical science, higher education, and cosmetic surgery, they can spend all their money and still grow richer. Wall Street magic will make them wealthier. The health industry's products will make them healthier. Too many will soon discover that their rock-candy mountains will melt under the weight of mortgage payments and credit card deficits that remain after the party is over.

To put all this in another way: It takes a *negative* savings rate, *expanding credit* to incredible levels, and *excessive* government spending *just to stand in one spot!* It doesn't take an MBA from Stanford to figure out that the Red Queen had it just right: "Here, you see, it takes all the running you can do, to keep in the same place. If you want to get somewhere else, you must run at least twice as fast as that!" And that is exactly what most families in the United States are doing—going further and faster into debt just to stand still in the same place.

Alice was learning

But Alice learned something more that we all will learn, sooner or later. She was on her way to the Garden of Live Flowers: "I should see the garden far better," said Alice to herself, "if I could get to the top of that hill: and here's a path that leads straight to it—at least, no, it doesn't do *that* ..." (after going a few yards along the path, and turning several sharp corners), "... but I suppose it will at last. But how curiously it twists! It's more like a corkscrew than a path! Well, *this* turn goes to the hill, I suppose—no, it doesn't! This goes straight back to the house! Well, then, I'll try it the other way.

"And so she did: wandering up and down, and trying turn after turn, but always coming back to the house, do what she would. Indeed, once, when she turned a corner rather more quickly than usual, she ran against it before she could stop herself."[3]

Lesson No. 1: In Alice's world, as in our world, forward movements most often take people back to their starting point; and rapid movements, whether in Wonderland or in the 21st century, can cause very abrupt stops.

Lesson No. 2: Alice found a way out, but financial and political leaders today are trapped with unintended consequences. Most countries are in the same fix as the United States: We can choose between hyperinflation (continue the same policies that got us where we are today) and deflation (slow down the economy with higher interest rates plus reduction in government spending). The problem before the Federal Reserve Bank is the same as Alice's—if we cannot run fast enough, our economy will implode (deflate). But if we run too fast, the value of the dollar (in precarious shape now) will come to a very sharp stop. Foreign governments will yank their billions out of the U.S. treasury; federal and state governments will have no choice but to rapidly increase taxes and swiftly reduce Medicare, grants, and other governmental assistance programs. Life as we have known it for half a century will come to a halt, abruptly!

Perhaps this is why Dan Blatt wrote recently: "Great acceleration toward the end is a common property of financial crises—most of which can seem manageable for months or years before the period of acceleration begin. While the impending crises themselves are often easily discernible by perceptive observers, predicting the onset of acceleration can be very difficult."[4]

---

3. Ibid., 139

4. *Strategic Investment,* March 3, 2005.

Or why David Walker, Comptroller General of the United States, said only a few months ago that the United States can be likened to Rome before the fall of the empire. Its financial condition is "worse than advertised" and it has a "broken business model. It faces deficits in its budget, its balance of payments, its savings— and its leadership."[5]

On another occasion, Paul Volcker said: "Under the placid surface, there are disturbing trends: huge imbalances, disequilibria, risks—call them what you will. Altogether the circumstances seem to me as dangerous and intractable as any I can remember, and I can remember quite a lot."[6]

Choke Points

What are some of the choke points that these financial leaders see on the near horizon?

In just one area alone, they are calling it "Petrocalypse Now!" Everyone on this planet will be directly affected. No one can deny, if they are serious, that global oil production is virtually equal to global oil demand! That means virtually no room for anything but maximum output, all day, every day—with no disasters, no civil wars, etc.

So what happens if China continues to demand its projected 15 percent increase in 2006 or if India's booming car market thirsts for another 48 percent increase in 2006. *System overload!*

But let's look at it another way: What could hamper the near 100-percent production capacity of the moment? Plenty!

▶ Killer hurricanes are predicted in the Gulf of Mexico in 2006. We still are not back to pre-Katrina production and that hurricane put only three percent of the 5,000 offshore rigs in the Gulf out of commission—and that was only a Category 4 hurricane! Imagine what a Category 5 hurricane could do!

▶ China, leading the exploding Asian demand, accounts for 40 percent of global oil growth since 2000; that's seven times faster

---

5. *USA Today,* November 14, 2005

6. *Strategic Investment,* May 1, 2005.

than the United States. In addition, China is outmaneuvering the United States in securing oil deals around the world, in such countries as Gabon, Nigeria, Brazil, Canada, Iran, and Venezuela.

▶ Global political tensions have never been so fragile and volatile. When the president of Iran calls for the "disgraceful blot" called Israel to be "wiped off the map," the price of oil goes up on the world market. Never mind that Iran pumps a lot of oil for the world, it also controls the critical Strait of Hormuz, through which 40 percent of the world's oil travels. It could be shut down over night!

▶ Iraq, a huge supplier of oil (when it restores some semblance of domestic tranquility), is a sitting target for Iran to move in and become king of the world's largest combined oil reserves. The United States, after billions of dollars to change regimes, has not bought a single barrel of its oil! The influx of foreign Islamo-fascist insurgent terrorists will postpone that dream. They shut down one oil facility per week now and it takes time and money to rebuild each one!

▶ Venezuela, long-time energy ally of the United States, as we write, is in the midst of anti-U.S. sentiment and is actively pursuing new relationships with China, jeopardizing the much-needed oil supply to the United States.

▶ Saudi Arabia, long-time pro-Americans (royal family), is ripe for an internal regime change, especially by the Osama bin Laden factions, a hero to many Saudis. After all, 55 percent of the resistance in Iraq is from Saudi Arabia!

▶ Potential terrorist attacks cloud all political as well as energy planners. Attacks thousands of miles away from the United States could paralyze this country's economy, as well as the world's. Let's look at some of these physical choke points:

◆ The Bab el–Mandab—a waterway that connects the Red Sea with the Gulf of Aden and Arabian Sea, through which about three million barrels per day pass—already a target for further attacks by Islamo-fascists.

◆ The Strait of Hormuz—a two-mile wide oil transit bottleneck through which 15 million barrels-per-day flow; that is, 40 percent of the world's oil exports!

♦ The Suez Canal and Sumed Pipeline—two oil chokepoints, where the Red Sea connects with the lower Mediterranean, combine for about 3.8 million barrels per day of oil, much marked for America. Sinking one super tanker in the canal would shut down this vital artery indefinitely.

What does all this mean?

What could all this mean *overnight?* Hard to remember, perhaps, but only a year ago in early 2005, crude oil was selling for $38 a barrel, now over $70; and unleaded gasoline, a little over $2.20—today, close to $3.00! But if even one out of the list of chokepoints I have mentioned happens, most economists agree we would face $150-per barrel for crude oil, $5.32 per gallon of gas, a 28-percent drop in the S&P 500 (which spells retirement investments for millions), massive unemployment, and a major recession. Are you ready for all that?

Although we have been focusing on the United States, the same economic problems are sweeping over European countries. Start with France and Germany with an unemployment rate twice that of the United States, plus government budgets that are out of control.

France has tried to waltz a plan that would encourage employers to hire young workers, but with the provision that anyone could be fired after two years for incompetence or any other reason that the employer thought necessary. But massive demonstrations in early 2006 virtually shut down Paris and other cities because the young want guaranteed jobs forever with no chance to be fired! One of the young marchers said, "We cannot see a future where we will be able to live as well as our parents. We are all afraid of the future—and we are not alone."[7]

World Fears

Experts do not foresee this concern going away. They see these marchers as a reflection not only of French fears over "needed

---

7. *Sacramento Bee*, April 11, 2006.

economic restructuring," but also of similar worries throughout Western Europe.

"France is a front-runner, but the tendencies exist everywhere," said Rob Boudewijn, an expert on European culture at the Clingendael Institute, a Dutch research center. "Europe hasn't been this desperate since the postwar period. People are feeling lost in an ever-growing European Union. They feel that economically they've already lost to China, and they have no idea where they fit into the world anymore."[8]

The basic problem is that socialistic countries are beginning to see on a massive scale that equal opportunity and equal outcomes are incompatible concepts—somebody has to pay somewhere. The source of the European malaise and fear is "recognition that change must come to an economic system that enjoys its long guaranteed cradle-to-grave government services, employment security, and benefits such as six-week vacations and large pensions. European businesses complain that they no longer can compete with foreign companies whose workers don't demand such perquisites."

Richard Whitman, an expert on European politics at Bath University in England, said: "This is a top-to-bottom problem in France. It is not a mood or a moment, it is a deeply felt resentment for the government, for the changes that are coming."[9]

Eric Thode, a labor economist at the German Bertelsmann Foundation, adds that the problem is not only the socialistic principles that now are strangling European countries, but also the consequences of uncontrolled immigration and globalization. Industrial jobs, across Europe as well as in the United States, have been flowing to less expensive labor markets, especially in Asia and Eastern Europe. As more jobs vanish, the financial underpinnings of European welfare states begin to crumble.

Thode further said that the "problems were just as great in

---

8. Ibid.

9. Ibid.

Germany, the Netherlands, and Italy, among other nations. The French simply are the quickest into the streets."[10]

Eating One's Tail

Sometime around 1600 B.C., the Egyptians created the image of a serpent devouring its own tail. Hundreds of years later, the Greeks gave the serpent a name: "Ouroboros." Some call the image a symbol of nature throughout the universe—creation out of destruction, life out of death—the Ouroboros eats its own tail to sustain its life.

To me, the Ouroboros is a symbol of what is happening in developing countries everywhere—homeowners are feeling "full" with the refinancing of their homes, pulling out equity for a new car, a swimming pool, more vacations, and the latest facial or tummy tuck. But they are eating their own tail to stay financially alive, even for only a little while.

How much of their tail can the people of this world eat before reality sets in? Some of this new form of gorging on the tail of the United States is the astounding rise of the "cult of the victim." In the last 60 years, young people have been taught that their government should pay the bills of anyone afflicted by hardship. The "cult of the victim" permeates political action and social expectation of western civilization—a remarkable tsunami overtaking traditional values and common sense. So many people have been taught that every manifestation of even perceived misfortune, incompetence, or underachievement might become a financial asset. After decades of government funding to subsidize failure and/or irresponsibility, we teach young people that failure can also become a personal asset.

What is the future of those caught in the "cult of the victim?" Their cries will not go away, especially when they have been excused for years in their school opportunities with inflated grades and unwarranted diplomas. Or excused for a dozen "reasons" when unwilling to take jobs that required hard work. When the government runs out of money or ideas to maintain the "cult of the victim," blood will flow in the streets.

---

10. Ibid.

Entitlement Cult

The same reasoning can be applied to the "entitlement cult." Americans in the last generation have been taught that life has always been this way—the government exists to provide for every facet of their lives. For nearly 200 years, not so! But today many, rich and poor, depend on the government for all kinds of services known as "entitlements."

That is why a balanced budget is an elusive phantom. The problem is that people rationalize that they have paid for their entitlements! But in reality, most entitlement beneficiaries will receive far more than they ever paid into the system. This includes Social Security and Medicare, but few want to know the truth. The money they are receiving is only borrowed to be paid back by the next generation—and that only by increased taxation. The Ouroboros is eating its own tail.[11]

I know you are asking, "What does all this have to do with Revelation 18:11, 17, the main theme of this chapter?" John the Revelator is describing a last-day scenario when the economy of the world and the world's merchants play a significant role in international turmoil. It is never been this late before.

In this chapter, we have briefly flown over the current economic/political distress in the United States and other Western countries. The East is awakening and falling into the same fragile instability.

Parallel with Germany in 1930s

Thoughtful historians are noticing the striking parallel between growing volatility in the West to the economic crisis that possessed Germany in the 1920s and 1930s. One-third of German's workforce unemployed, drastic inflation, food scarce, national shame—all

---

11. As I write this chapter on April 14, 2006, the exodus of dollars from the U.S. Treasury back to foreign countries as well as back to big institutions has begun, big time. The U.S. 10-year bond is the key to price borrowing in the American economy with ripple effects throughout the global system. Senior economists say that this sudden rise in 10-year yields risk tipping the US economy (and others) into a downturn. What does this mean? Higher interest rates for buying anything, including houses, cars, etc., and higher rates for those who bought homes with their ARMs.

this made possible Hitler's rise to power. Wheelbarrows full of paper money were hurried to the grocery store to buy a few loaves of bread before the price would rise again. Hitler promised to reverse those awful conditions, blaming everything on the Jews and Communists.

America and other industrialized nations have few people who dare to explain to their countrymen that we are fast approaching the tipping point. American must *borrow* each year to pay even the interest on its debt, never mind pay off the principal. What kind of security is that? Of course, the country could declare bankruptcy, but it doesn't take long to picture what happens then. People will indeed march in the streets, but it won't be merely flag waving. Every nation in the world is facing the same choices.

Heraclitus, around 500 B.C., famously said that we "cannot step into the same river twice." But citizens of the world today think they can! They persist in believing that nothing can possibly change—America's industry and science has always led the world; the American dollar has always been the world's reserve currency.

But with billions of hungry workers in Asia, never mind hundreds of thousands in Mexico, eager for American jobs, new waters are flowing into the river, every second. Such thinking that stocks and home prices will always go up, that the government will also fund whatever is needed, will soon come to a shivering halt. Why?

Labor wants its jobs protected. Business wants its markets protected. Politicians want their careers protected. At the same time, most everyone wants the low prices at Wal-Mart protected. This kind of balancing act is unsustainable—something like squaring a circle.

What has been the accelerating force that has brought us to the tipping point? Many say it is globalization—a concept that just didn't pop up without a lot of thought! Immediately one can see how globalization has redistributed the labor market. For instance, call your telephone company and somebody in India will answer— if one can understand the English accent!

Globalization is the open secret of the incredible worldwide expansion of Wal-Mart and why merchandise can be bought at this giant for most reasonable prices. But the merchandise was mostly made in other countries with cheaper labor.

But the dark side of globalization is the interconnection of international corporations in all the major countries. Economic disasters in one country will ripple through the global market. All the various potential troubles mentioned earlier in this chapter will be only amplified in a global economy. Western world governments, and soon Eastern countries, are experiencing change and upheaval like never before. Decades of interlocking partnerships are feeling the galloping stress that leaves no room for a solution—bloated governments will face what some economists are calling "punctuated equilibrium." Another definition for bankruptcy!

We end this brief overview of pending international economic crises by linking two dramatic predictions: Revelation 18:11, 17— *"And the merchants of the earth will weep and mourn over her, for no one buys their merchandise anymore. ... For in one hour such great riches came to nothing."*

Now think of a familiar comment made by Ellen White in *Testimonies,* vol. 9, p. 13: "There are not many, even among educators and statesmen, who comprehend the causes that underlie the present state of society. Those who hold the reins of government are not able to solve the problem of moral corruption, poverty, pauperism, and increasing crime. They are struggling in vain to place business operations on a more secure basis" (emphasis added).

Reread this prediction again, slowly. Sounds like today's newspaper, doesn't it! Every word of that prediction is being played out as time merges into those days when merchants of the earth will have nothing to sell because no one has money to buy. All the "great riches" of the world come "to nothing."

Perhaps some are asking, "What does an economic collapse have to do with the Second Advent? Answer: The coming international economic collapse, coupled with natural disasters, will drive governments to find scapegoats for the escalating calamities.

Future Scenario

The religious card will be played. Something like this will be said by perhaps the president of the United States: "We are in an enormous crisis. We need unity like never before. We need to restore our common values, our religious roots. We need fewer divisions, less hate talk. In fact, we are going to outlaw any group talking negatively about anyone else. This is a time to come together and fulfill the American dream. Remember, 'Righteousness exalted a nation.' Let's restore peace to our communities, at least for one day of the week. Let's restore America to the way it used to be."

Bingo! Sunday will be the day of choice and the plea for tolerance and national unity will trump all negative talk about anyone's sexual orientation, ethnic origin or religious beliefs.

So what, someone may ask? These unprecedented conditions we have been reviewing in these pages will soon compel frightened citizens to enact strict government laws that will evaporate the basic freedoms this country was founded on. For instance, no longer will it be permissible to argue for which day is the Sabbath or to point out who changed it—that will be divisive and subject to rapid, legal incarceration.

Bottom line——such a time will come when loyal, patriotic citizens will not be able to buy or sell. And if they continue to be divisive with their appeal to freedom as guaranteed in the Constitution, Revelation 13 comes in to play. Verse fifteen predicts that the law will say that they should be killed! We are not there yet, but the stage is surely being set. "It has never been this late before."

Does anyone still doubt the accuracy of the three predictions that we have just reviewed—Revelation 12, 13, 18 and *Testimonies,* volume 9?

♦ CHAPTER THREE ♦

All the World Wondered!

I n our last chapter, we noted briefly that the interlocking of international business would most likely cause the coming financial collapse of nations around the world. The shivering halt to
the worldwide mania that "good times" will last forever (even on
borrowed money) is made more probable by the steel spider web
of globalization. What happens in one country causes a developing ripple in others.

But this coming financial disaster will eventually be linked
with another kind of interlocking global strategy—a strategy that
also includes the whole world. We have only a small space in this
chapter to unfold what we mean. Here we can only tease with
several observations.

Most of us remember President George Herbert Walker Bush's
State of the Union address before the U.S. Congress on January 29,
1991! A few days before, Congress had voted for war against Iraq.
In his speech, Bush said: "What is at stake is more than one small
country, it is a big idea—*a new world order*, where diverse nations are
drawn together in common cause to achieve the universal aspirations
of mankind: peace and security, freedom, and the rule of law. Such is a
world worthy of our struggle, and worthy of our children's future!"

A "new world order"! For many Americans, that sounded like something describing millennial bliss! However, the phrase "new world order" has been used thousands of times in the last century by highly placed leaders in education, industry, banking, the media, and politics. Just to go down the list would make another book. In a special way, it became the mantra during the 1960–1980 for those pushing "Values Clarification" and "Outcome–based Education"—a veritable hurricane shift in the public school system in the United States.

On July 26, 1968 (Associated Press report), Nelson Rockefeller pledged in his run for the presidency that "as President, he would work toward international creation of a *new world order.*" In 1968, Rockefeller published his book *The Future of Federalism*, a compelling outline of his mantra, *new world order,* that the older is crumbling and there is a "new and free order struggling to be born." He went on to say that at present there was a:

> "fever of nationalism ... [but] the nation-state is becoming less and less competent to perform its international political tasks. ... These are some of the reasons pressing us to lead vigorously toward the true building of a *new world order* ... [with] voluntary service ... and our dedicated faith in the brotherhood of all mankind. ... Sooner perhaps than we may realize ... there will evolve the bases for a federal structure of the free world" (emphasis supplied).

In 1975, 32 Senators and 92 Representatives signed "A Declaration of Interdependence," written by the distinguished historian Henry Steele Commager, that stated: "We must join with others to bring forth a *new world order.* ... Narrow notions of national sovereignty must not be permitted to curtail that obligation."

In his address to the United Nations on December 7, 1988, Mikhail Gorbachev called for mutual consensus: "World progress is only possible through a search for universal human consensus as we move toward a *new world order.*"

On May 12, 1989, President George H.W. Bush stated that the United States is ready to welcome the Soviet Union "back into the *world order.*"

On September 11, 1990, months before the Gulf War began,

President Bush emphasized his strategy: "The crisis in the Persian Gulf offers a rare opportunity to move toward an historic period of cooperation. Out of these troubled times ... *a new world order* can emerge in which the nations of the world, east and west, north and south, can prosper and live in harmony. ... Today the *new world* is struggling to be born."

A remarkable peek into how all this gets circulated into the bloodstream of Americans was revealed by David Rockefeller at the Council on Foreign Relations in June 1991. Sixty-five prestigious members of government, labor, academia, the media, military, and the professions from nine countries heard Rockefeller say: "We are grateful to the *Washington Post, The New York Times, Time Magazine,* and other great publications whose directors have attended our meetings and respected their promises of discretion for almost 40 years. It would have been impossible for us to develop our plan for the world if we had been subjected to the lights of publicity during those years. But the world is now more sophisticated and prepared to march towards a world government. The supranational sovereignty of an intellectual elite and world bankers is surely preferable to the national auto-determination practiced in past centuries."

It might take a couple of deep breaths and several re-reads of that paragraph to grasp what Rockefeller is revealing.

As if on cue, *Time* magazine published on July 20, 1992, Strobe Talbott's *The Birth of the Global Nation* in which he wrote: "All countries are basically social arrangements. ... No matter how permanent or even sacred they may seem at any one time, in fact they are all artificial and temporary. ... Perhaps national sovereignty wasn't such a great idea after all. ... But it has taken the events in our own wondrous and terrible century to clinch the case for *world government.*" Talbott was soon appointed as the number two person behind Warren Christopher where he continued his sharp focus.

The State of the World Forum, in the fall of 1995, held its meeting at the Presidio in San Francisco attended by the who's who of the world, including Margaret Thatcher, Maurice Strong, George H.W. Bush, and Mikhail Gorbachev. The term "global governance" was now being used instead of "new world order."

A year later, the United Nations published a 420-page report, *Our Global Neighborhood*, that laid out the plans for "global governance" in the years ahead.

The point is: It might be taking somewhat longer to achieve the "new world" dream that key world leaders have been working on behind the scenes for decades. But the trajectory has never been sharper than today. One has to be blind and deaf not to detect its forward motion in politics, social programs, financial enterprises, as well as in religious confederations never thought possible a generation ago.

But the "new world order" strategy has its mirror image, a linkage that will soon become more evident. This parallel movement found enormous traction in the rise of Pope John II, beginning even before he became the 263rd successor to Peter the Apostle, as his Catholic friends would call it.

In 1976, the Polish archbishop from Krakow, Karol Wojtyla, spoke before a New York City audience and said: "We are now standing in the face of the greatest historical confrontation humanity has gone through ... a test of 2,000 years of culture and Christian civilization, with all of its consequences for human dignity, individual rights, and the rights of nations." But, he continued, "Wide circles of American society and wide circles of the Christian community do not realize this fully."[1]

Of course, the soon-to-be pope was speaking of the three major global powers that sooner or later would meld into one—the Soviet Union under Mikhail Gorbachev, the United States led by Ronald Reagan, and the most deeply experienced major power, the Papacy.[2] Each in their time and now maintained in their successors

---

1. Malachi Martin, *The Keys of the Blood* (New York: Simon & Schuster, 1990), 16.

2. Ibid., 17. Martin observed that the "final contender in the competition for the new world over is not a single individual leader or a single institution or territory. It is a group of men who are united as one in power, mind and will for the purpose of achieving a single common goal: to be victorious in the competition for the new global hegemony."

had the same geopolitical aims; each had a grand design for world governance "that will replace the decaying nation system."

As a few short years passed, the grand design in the mind of Gorbachev faded, leaving only two world powers to lead the inexorable flow of "the new world order." In this flow, we can see the beginning of the fulfillment of the predictions in Revelation 13–18; now we see more clearly the endgame that will usher in the framework for the fulfilling of Revelation 17:13, when the nations of earth with "one mind" will give their power and authority to the power represented by the "beast." The global power recognized by all as the United States and the global power recognized by all as the Papacy join in common interests, with "one mind."

From the beginning of his pontificate in October 1978, Pope John Paul II astonished the world with his decision to become a decisive factor in determining the "new world order." He did it without press agents or a clever propaganda machine; he did it himself. In his first 12 years, he made 45 papal trips to 91 countries, giving a total of 1,559 speeches in 32 languages, being heard in the flesh or on audio-video hookups by more than 3.5 billion people.[3]

But what is even more astonishing, Pope John Paul never went as a casual tourist or a distinguished visitor. Hardly! He was formally received by the host government in a category far above a Billy Graham or Dalai Lama, or any other religious leader. In his Vatican home, 120 diplomatic missions were sent there by their governments. Every comment on his thoughts and acts was front-page news. And no government complained or tried to argue with him. No one gave him the right to speak as religious authority on all things political and moral—he simply assumed it.

Always cementing these international relationships, yet always waiting. For what? He had been waiting "for an event that will fission human history, splitting the immediate past from the oncoming future. It will be an event on public view in the skies, in the oceans, and on the continental landmasses of this planet. It will particularly involve our human sun, which every day lights up and shines upon the valleys, the mountains and the plains of this

---

3. Ibid., 490

earth for our eyes. But on the day of this event, it will not appear merely as the master star of our so-called solar system. Rather, it will be seen as the circumambient glory of the Woman whom the apostle describes as 'clothed with the sun' and giving birth to 'a child who will rule the nations with a scepter of iron.' "[4]

One of the driving forces in Pope John Paul's life was that he took the Fatima[5] message personally. He believed that he was designated God's Servant in the divine plan and providence, that he had an unpleasant message and, perhaps, a thankless job. He strongly felt that he had to warn the world of his convictions that human catastrophe on a world scale was impending. However, he knew it would not come without a warning, but that only those with renewed hearts would "recognize it for what it is and make preparations for the tribulations that will follow."[6]

Let's take a further overview of Pope John Paul's record since 1978 until he died in 2005:

▶ June 7, 1982. President Ronald Reagan and Pope John Paul II talked for 50 minutes in the Vatican Library, later called "one of the great secret alliances of all time"; its purpose— the collapse of the Soviet Union and the encouragement of reform movements in Hungary, Czechoslovakia, and the Pope's beloved Poland.[7]

---

4. Ibid., 639

5. On October 13, 1917, three peasant girls claimed they saw and heard Mary, our Lord's mother, who gave them three messages. The first two messages were soon revealed, but the third was not to be opened until 1960. The first put the church, as well as society in general, on notice that they were heading toward the eternal punishment of hell. The second is understood as a prophecy of World War II and that Russia would spread evil throughout the world and many would suffer and die. The third message, written by the surviving child who became a Carmelite nun in Coimbra, Portugal, was opened by John XXIII who felt it had no relevancy to his pontificate, so it was returned to its hiding place in the Pope's quarters until Pope John Paul II made it available. The message referred to physical and spiritual chastisement of the nations of the world, including Roman Catholics—all of which may be mitigated by prayers to "Mother Mary."—Ibid., 627-233.

6. Ibid., 637.

7. *Time*, February 24, 1992, 28.

▶ 1984. On September 22, 1983, Senator Dan Quayle appealed to the U.S. Senate: "Under the courageous leadership of Pope John Paul II, the Vatican State has assumed its rightful place in the world as an international voice. It is only right that this country show its respect for the Vatican by diplomatically recognizing it as a world state."[8] In the following year, President Reagan appointed the first ambassador to the Vatican (not a personal representative), thereby recognizing for the first time the political significance of the central government of the Roman Catholic Church.[9]

▶ December 1, 1989. Vatican Summit—President Gorbachev and the Pope represented two contrasting visions of a "new world order." When Gorbachev addressed John Paul II as "the world's highest moral authority," he recognized that he was not dealing with a "straw man."[10] Gorbachev, several years later, said: "I have carried on an intensive correspondence with Pope John Paul II since we met at the Vatican in December 1989. And I think ours will be an ongoing dialogue. ... I am certain that the actions undertaken by John Paul II will play an enormous political role now that profound changes have occurred in European history."[11]

▶ 1989. Collapse of the Soviet Union was due primarily to the "great secret alliance"; and "the rush to freedom in Eastern Europe is a sweet victory for John Paul II."[12] "While Gorbachev's hands-off policies were the immediate cause of the chain reaction of liberty that has swept over Eastern Europe in the past few months, John Paul deserves much of the longer-range credit."[13]

---

8. Pope John Paul II "insists that men have no reliable hope of creating a viable geopolitical system unless it is on the basis of Roman Catholic Christianity."—Martin, op. cit., 492.

9. Thomas P. Melady, *The Ambassador's Story—The United States and the Vatican in World Affairs* (Huntington, IN: Our Sunday Visitor, Inc., 1994), 50.

10. Ibid., 491.

11. *South Bend Tribune*, March 9, 1992, cited in Dwight K. Nelson, Countdown to the Showdown (Fallbrook, CA: Hart Research Center, 1992), 40, 41.

12. *Life*, December 1989.

13. *Time*, December 4, 1989

▶ May 1, 1991. Pope John Paul II's *Centesimus Annus* (The Hundredth Year: On the Hundredth Anniversary of *Rerum Novarum*). A remarkable *restatement* of Pope Leo XIII's overview of the rights of workers worldwide and how various government forms deny these rights. Ironically, both popes argue for religious liberty for all and yet call for government recognition of Sunday as the workers' day of rest and worship.[14]

▶ February 24, 1992. Cover story of *Time* magazine: "Holy Alliance—How Reagan and the Pope conspired to assist Poland's Solidarity movement and hasten the demise of Communism: An Investigative Report." Carl Bernstein reported, "Step by reluctant step, the Soviets and the communist government of Poland bowed to the moral, economic, and political presence imposed by the Pope and the President."[15]

▶ Summer, 1993, Colorado Youth Festival. After the Pope's visit to Colorado, the Vatican sensed a new opportunity to forge with the United States a plan to exert a "moral authority in world affairs."[16]

▶ January 9, 1994. Israel and Vatican sign a "fundamental agreement" after 45 years of troubled relationships. Israeli diplomats say that "the agreement acknowledges the inherent stake of the Catholic Church in the Holy Land; the church is not a guest ... but part and parcel of the reality of Israel."[17]

▶ March 29, 1994. "Evangelicals and Catholics Together: The Christian Mission in the 3rd Millennium"—a meeting and document that many say reversed 500 years of church history. To imply that both sides preach the same Christ, understand authority and the "church" the same way, or hold the same understanding of "justification by grace through faith" is the test of credulity, but no matter: Both sides "contend together"

---

14. www.ewtn.com/library/ENCYC/JP2HUNDR.HTM -

15. *Time*, February 24, 1992, 24-35.

16. Alan Cowell in *New York Times*, August 18, 1993

17. *National Catholic Register*, January 9, 16, 1994.

to uphold "sanctity of life, family values, parental choice in education, moral standards in society, and democratic institutions worldwide." Further, "We affirm that a common set of core values is found in the teachings of religions, and that these form the basis of a global ethic ... and which are the conditions for a sustainable world order." New phrases such as the church being responsible "for the right ordering of civil society" are more than interesting. Further, they agree that "it is neither theologically legitimate nor a prudent use of resources" to proselytize among active members of another Christian community.[18] As many say, "an historic moment."[19] Indeed!

▶ October 16, 1994. Israel's first ambassador to the Vatican said his meeting with the Pope opened a "new epoch of cooperation." The Pope expressed his long-standing request for "international guarantees" to protect the "sacred character of Jerusalem," a city sacred to Christians, Muslims, and Jews.[20]

▶ November 10, 1994. In his apostolic letter, *"Tertio Millennio Adventiente"* ("The Coming Third Millennium"), the Pope built on the new era opened up by Vatican II—the "profound renewal" that opened up the Catholic church to other Christians, the focus of each year from 1995 to the Grand Jubilee year of 2000, symbolic journeys to Bethlehem, Jerusalem, and Mount Sinai "as a means of furthering dialogue with Jews and the followers of Islam, and to arranging similar meetings elsewhere with the leaders of the great world religions." The time between 1994 and 2000 were busy indeed as the Pope fulfilled the plans laid out in this letter.[21]

---

18. Full text of the document in Clifford Goldstein *One Nation Under God?* (Boise, ID: PPPA, 1996), 143-160. See "Catholics and Evangelicals in the Trenches," *Christianity Today,* May 16, 1994; J. I. Packer, "Why I Signed It," Ibid., December 12, 1994.

19. John White, former president of the National Association of Evangelicals, *USA Today,* March 30, 1994. On March 29, 1994, *The Oregonian* summarized an Associated Press story with subtitle: "Catholic and evangelical leaders vow to join in a common bond to work toward shared values."

20. *National Catholic Register,* October 16, 1994.

21. *National Catholic Register,* December 11, 1994.

▶ November 13, 1994. In his column, "Why Catholics Are Our Allies," Charles Colson wrote (carrying through the agenda developing for decades): "Believers on the front lines, battling issues such as abortion, pornography, and threats to religious liberty, find themselves sharing foxholes with conservatives across denominational lines—forging what theologian Timothy George calls 'an ecumenism of the trenches.'... The great divides within Christendom no longer fall along denominational lines but between conservatives and liberals *within* denominations. ... Let's be certain that we are firing our polemical rifles against the enemy, not against those fighting in the trenches alongside us in defense of the Truth." [22]

▶ January 2, 1995. *Time* –"John Paul II, Man of the Year." "People who see him—and countless millions have—do not forget him. His appearances generate electricity unmatched by anyone else on earth. ... When he talks, it is not only to his flock of nearly a billion; he expects the world to listen. ... In a year when so many people lamented the decline in moral values or made excuses for bad behavior, Pope John Paul II forcefully set forth his vision of the good life and urged the world to follow it. ... John Paul's impact on the world has already been enormous, ranging from the global to the personal. ... With increased urgency ... John Paul presented himself, the defender of Roman Catholic doctrine, as a moral compass for believers and nonbelievers alike. ... Billy Graham said, 'He's been the strong conscience of the whole Christian world.' " [23]

▶ January 21,1995. In Colombo, Sri Lanka, "Pope John Paul II

---

22. *Christianity Today,* November 14, 1994. One of the books I read in my early ministry was Paul Blanchard's *American Freedom and Catholic Power* (Boston: The Beacon Press, 1949). A breathtaking book, he revealed the strategy of how the Catholic Church would eventually dominate the politics of the United States, long before others were writing with such precision. How would they do this? The Church would turn the eyes of conservative Protestant America toward common values such as birth control, abortion, family values, and control of education. In that same year, America saw a very effective advertising campaign sponsored by the Knights of Columbus to remove misconceptions about Rome.—*EndTime Issues,* September 1999.

23. December 26, 1994 /January 2, 1995, 53, 54.

ended an exhausting Asian tour with a call for the world's great religions to unite on behalf of shared moral values."[24]

▶ May 30, 1995. Papal encyclical, *"Ut Unum Sin"* (That They May be One), laid out, unambiguously, a powerful strategy for church unity, on one front to develop a non-confrontational relationship with Islam, on the other, throughout the Christian world. This document committed the Roman Catholic Church to full communion with the Eastern Orthodox Church, that unity is more important than jurisdiction. And to the Protestant churches, he reminded them that the "Petrine ministry" belongs to all Christians, whether they recognize it or not.[25]

▶ October 7, 1995. When Pope John Paul II presided at a mass in New York's Central Park, an estimated 125,000 people turned out to see, not only the leader of the world's largest Christian church, but also an ecumenical procession of Protestant, Orthodox, and other non–Catholic religious leaders, including "political power broker Pat Robertson at the head of the line." After the mass and an intimate visit with the Pope, Robertson "insisted that a new day is dawning in the relationship between conservative Protestants and traditional Roman Catholics."[26]

▶ July 7, 1998. *"Dies Domini"*("Lord's Day"). From the first sentence, the Pope focused on "the Lord's Day—as Sunday was called from Apostolic times." The entire document is amazing in subtle mal-exegesis, but very persuasive to the surface reader. Outlined in 87 sections, note the following: "62. It is the duty of Christians therefore to remember that, although the practices of the Jewish Sabbath are gone, surpassed as they are by the 'fulfillment' which Sunday brings, the underlying reasons for keeping 'the Lord's Day' holy—inscribed solemnly in the Ten Commandments—remain valid, though they need

24. *The Orlando Sentinel,* January 22, 1995.

25. www.vatican.va/holy_father/John_Paul_II/encyclicals/document. Richard John Neuhaus, *The Wall Street Journal,* July 6, 1995.

26. Joseph L. Conn, "Papal Blessing?" *Church and State,* November, 1995.

to be reinterpreted in the light of the theology and spirituality of Sunday. ... 66. ... My predecessor Pope Leo XIII in his Encyclical *Rerum Novarum* spoke of Sunday rest as a worker's right which the State must guarantee. ... 67. ... Therefore, also in the particular circumstances of our own time, Christians will naturally strive to ensure that civil legislations respects their duty to keep Sunday holy."[27]

▶ October 27, 28, 1998. Archbishop Lean–Louis Tauran said that Jerusalem "has long been at the center of the Holy See's concerns and one of its top priorities for international action. ... The Holy See believes in the importance of extending representation at the negotiating table in order to be sure that no aspect of the problem is overlooked."[28]

▶ October 30, 1998. A nine-page document signed by Cardinal Ratzinger (Pope Benedict XVI since 2005) emphasized that popes alone can determine the limits of those at the negotiating table (see above). Publicly, Ratzinger said, "It is clear that only the pope ... as successor of Peter, has the authority and the competence to speak the last word on the means of exercising the pastoral ministry of the universal truth." "The papacy," he said, "is not an office of the presidency ... and cannot be conceived of as a type of political monarchy."[29]

▶ May 12, 1999. Anglican-Roman Catholic International Commission (18 Anglican and Roman Catholic members), continuing a dialogue that began in 1981, published an agreed statement with amazing convergences such as: "62. An experience of universal primacy of this kind would confirm two particular conclusions we have reached: 1) that Anglicans be open to and desire a recovery and re-reception under certain clear conditions of the exercise of universal primacy by the Bishop of Rome; and 2) that Roman Catholics be open to and desire a re-reception of the exercise of primacy by the

---

27. www.vatican.va/holly_father/john_paul_IIapostolic_letters/enframe28_en.htm.

28. www.vatican.va

29. Associated Press, 10/30/98 1:12, PM

Bishop of Rome and the offering of such a ministry to the whole Church of God."[30]

▶ September 1, 1999. March 8, 12, 23, 2000. Pope apologizes for "its past mistakes ... and to ask pardon for the historical offenses of its sons [sic]. ... The wounds of the past, for which both sides share the guilt, continue to be a scandal for the world." Auxiliary Archbishop Rino Fisichella of Rome said of the March 12 meeting in St. Peter's: "Pope John Paul II wanted to give a complete global vision, making references to circumstances of the past, but without focusing on details out of respect for history. ... The Church is not the one who has sinned, the sinners are Christians, and they have done so against the Church, the bride of Christ."[31]

▶ October 31, 1999. In the spring of 2000, my wife and I visited Augsburg, Germany, with one purpose—to visit the Reformation Church in which the Confession of the Princes was presented to Charles V in 1530. D'Aubigné wrote that "this was destined to be the greatest day of the Reformation, and one of the most glorious in the history of Christianity and of mankind. ... The Confession of Augsburg will ever remain one of the masterpieces of the human mind enlightened by the Spirit

---

30. www.ewtn.corn/liberty/theology/arcicgh1 John Wilkins, editor of *The Tablet,* commented: "This 'Gift of Authority' now joins the other documents developed by this conference as an agenda in waiting. The commission's work is like a deposit in a bank. Its value will be evident when the time comes for it to be withdrawn for us." www.natcath.com/NCR_Online archives. Dr. George Carey, Archbishop of Canterbury said: "In a world torn apart by violence and division, Christians need urgently to be able to speak with a common voice, confident of the authority of the gospel of peace."— Oliver Poole, "Churches Agree Pope Has Overall Authority," BBCNews, May 13. www.antipas.org/magazine/articles, churches_agree_people.

31. *Zenit,—Rome,* March 12, 13, 2000. "John Paul has one foot in the dimension of history (where mess, error, violence, fanaticism, and stupidity flourish merrily) and the other in the dimension of eternity (where he must insist the holiness and infallibility of the church as the mystical body of Christ remain intact). It is awkward: How does infallibility own up to its fallibilities and yet remain infallible? The Pope's solution: by being vague about the actual sins and by attributing them, in any case, to men and women who are Catholics and not to the Catholic Church itself."—Lance Morrow, "Is it Enough to Be Sorry?" *Times,* March 27, 2000.

of God."[32] But on October 31, 1999, in that very church, 482 years to the day after Martin Luther had nailed those 95 theses to the door of the village church in Wittenberg, the Lutheran World Federation (not including all branches of the Lutheran Church, such as the Missouri Synod) signed with the Roman Catholics the Joint Declaration on the Doctrine of Justification, after 30 years of consultation.

What is so amazing is that 400 years before, Protestants and Catholics were in profound disagreement over the doctrine of justification, leading to vicious, deadly consequences. Just one more example of how diminished clarity of truth is today and how much "relationship" and "unity" have emerged as the most important issues for so many leading voices in modern Christianity.[33] All these thoughts blew through my mind as I sat solemnly in those same pews, where stalwart princes once put their lives on the line and where, 482 years later, "princes of the church" voted in the fog of their lost precision of thought.

▶ November 7, 1999. In New Delhi, India, Pope John Paul II, recognizing Catholicism's minority status in India, said that "no state, no group has the right to control either directly or indirectly a person's religious convictions ... or the respectful appeal of a particular religion to people's free conscience."[34]

▶ January 27, 2000. Congressional Gold Medal (USA): "To authorize a gold medal to be awarded on behalf of the Congress to Pope John II in recognition of his many and enduring contributions to peace and religious understanding, and for other purposes. ... The Congress finds that Pope John Paul II ... is recognized in the United States and abroad as a preeminent moral authority; has dedicated his Pontificate to the freedom and dignity of every individual human being and tirelessly traveled to the far reaches of the globe as an exemplar of faith;

---

32. J. H. Merle D'Aubigné, *History of the Reformation of the Sixteenth Century* (New York: Robert Carter and Brothers, 1875), bk. 14, chap. 7, 563, 566.

33. *Christianity Today,* October 25, 1999; www.tcsn.net/fbchurch/fb/cdecia.htm.

34. Associated Press, November 8, 1999.

has brought hope to millions of people all over the world oppressed by poverty, hunger, illness, and despair; transcending temporal politics, has used his moral authority to hasten the fall of godless totalitarian regimes, symbolized in the collapse of the Berlin wall; has promoted the inner peace of man as well as peace among mankind through his faith-inspired defense of justice; and has thrown open the doors of the Catholic Church, reconciling differences within Christendom as well as reaching out to the world's great religions."[35]

▶ June 5, 2000. President Putin asks Pope John Paul II for "help in gaining Russia's political and military integration in Europe." Putin called his stop "a very significant visit."[36]

▶ September 5, 2000. *Dominus Jesus*: A 36-page update from the Congregation for the Doctrine of the Faith, it rejects in unambiguous terms the notion that "one religion is as good as another," that the Catholic Church is "complementary" to other religions, and that Protestants, for example, are "Churches in the proper sense."[37]

▶ October 2000. Queen Elizabeth II, head of the church and state of England, visited Pope John Paul II and was "pleased to note the important progress that has been made in overcoming historic differences between Anglicans and Roman Catholics— as exemplified in particular by the meeting of Anglicans and Roman Catholics in Canada this year. I trust that we shall continue to advance along the path which leads to Christian unity."[38]

▶ January 6, 2001. The Pope's Apostolic Letter, "At the Beginning of the New Millennium," among other directives, emphasized the importance of Sunday as "a special day of faith, the day of the Risen Lord and of the gift of the Spirit, the true weekly

---

35. Internet: www.feds.com/basic_svc/public_law/106-175htm

36. CNN.com. June 5, 2000.

37. Catholic World News—Vatican Updates—09/05/2000; *Christianity Today,* September 11, 2000.

38. www.britain.it/royalvisit/3e.hdtm

Easter. ... We do not know what the new millennium has in store for us, but we are certain that it is safe in the hands of Christ, the 'King of kings and Lord of lords' (Rev. 19:16); and precisely by celebrating his Passover not just once a year but every Sunday, the Church will continue to show to every generation 'the true fulcrum of history, to which the mystery of the world's origin and its final destiny leads."[39]

▶ January 31, 2001. President Bush told 25 Catholic leaders that his interest was to "draw on Catholic wisdom and experience . ... I think you are seeing a historic and ground-breaking moment in the participation of Catholics in public life." Archbishop Caput, present for the dialogue, said Catholic social teaching is based on two pillars: dignity of the individual and commitment to the common good. Bush has often referred to the "common good" as an important administrative goal.[40]

▶ March 22, 2001. Washington, D.C.'s Pope John Paul II Cultural Center opened; first proposed for Krakow, Warsaw, or Rome but the Pope chose Washington, D.C., which he described as "the crossroads of the world."[41] "Cardinal Maida said there was no illusion that putting the center in Washington would precipitate an immediate change in the thinking of presidents, Supreme Court Justices, Members of Congress or other officials. ... But as we tell the story better, people will be affected by osmosis."[42]

▶ May 2001, the Pope, the first Catholic leader to enter the Umayyad Mosque in the Syrian capital of Damascus, participated in an organized prayer service. For Muslims, it is the oldest stone mosque in the world, while for Christians it is the alleged place where John the Baptist was buried. The Pope led in Christian prayers, while his Moslem counterpart,

39. www.vatican.va/holy_father/John_Paul_it/apost_letters/documents/

40. "Bush Meets With Catholics on Faith-based Initiatives," *National Catholic Register,* February 11-17, 2001.

41. Pat McCloskey, "Washington's New Pope John Paul II Cultural Center," *St. Anthony Messenger,* April 2001.

42. *The National Catholic Register,* October 26-November 1, 1997.

Sheikh Ahmed Kataro, led in Moslem prayers. By this dramatic act of worshiping in a mosque, the Pope underlined his commitment to work toward a rapprochement with the Muslims.

▶ September 2001, the Pope, in Almaty, Kazakhstan, 12 days after the horrors of September 11, renewed his commitment to work toward a new partnership with Moslems in his message to the predominantly Muslim nation of Kazakhstan. The Pope declared: " 'There is one God'. The Apostle proclaims before all else the absolute oneness of God. This is a truth which Christians inherited from the children of Israel and which they share with Muslims: it is faith in the one God, 'Lord of heaven and earth' (Luke 10:21), almighty and merciful. In the name of this one God, I turn to the people of deep and ancient religious traditions, the people of Kazakhstan." [43]

The Pope then appealed to both Muslims and Christians to work together to build a "civilization of love": "This 'logic of love' is what he [Jesus] holds out to us, asking us to live it above all through generosity to those in need. It is a logic that can bring together Christians and Muslims, and commit them to work together for the 'civilization of love.' It is a logic which overcomes all the cunning of this world and allows us to make true friends who will welcome us 'into the eternal dwelling-places' (Luke 16:9), into the 'homeland' of heaven."

▶ January 24, 2002. In Assisi, Italy, the Pope and more than 100 religious leaders from around the world, including Orthodox patriarchs, Jewish rabbis, grand muftis, sheikhs and other Muslim representatives, Buddhists and Shinto monks, Hindu leaders, Zoroastrians (whose adherents are mostly in India and Iran), leaders of traditional African religions, Protestant leaders, and 25 Roman Catholic cardinals and approximately 30 bishops shared in a day pursuing "authentic peace." Ending the day, the Pope lit a symbolic lamp of peace with the words: "Violence never again! War never again! Terrorism never again!

---

43. http://www.vatican.va/holy_father/john_paul_ii/homilies/2001/documents/ hf_jpii_hom_20010923_kazakhstan_astana_en.html

In God's name, may all religions bring upon earth justice and peace, forgiveness, life and love."[44]

▶ October 16, 2003. In celebrating Pope John Paul II's 25 years as leader of the Roman Catholic Church, Tracy Wilkinson of the *Lost Angeles Times* wrote: "This planet now is a very different place [compared to October 16, 1978], and John Paul II ... has had a hand in shaping events to a degree unrivaled by any other religious figure in modern history. His election on Oct. 16, 1978 'was itself a breaker of precedents,' the Jesuit magazine *America* said in an editorial this month, 'and ever since his election John Paul II's pontificate has been setting records that none of his predecessors could have imagined.'"[45]

▶April 2, 2005. Pope John Paul II died after holding "the chair of St. Peter" for 26 years. He had appeared on the cover of *Time* magazine—more than any other person, ever—16 times. President George W. Bush and his wife, Laura, made the following statement (in part): "Laura and I join people across the earth in mourning the passing of Pope John Paul II. The Catholic Church has lost its shepherd, the world has lost a champion of human freedom, and a good and faithful servant of God has been called home."

▶ President Bush then issued an executive order that the flag of the United States, "as a mark of respect for His Holiness, Pope John Paul II," shall be flown at half-mast on all federal government buildings throughout the United States and its territories until sunset of his interment. This order would include all United States embassies and other facilities abroad as well as all naval vessels.

At the Pope's funeral, three U.S. Presidents knelt for about five minutes in front of a pope's casket, heads bowed. More than 100 official delegations also attended, including four kings, five queens, and more than 70 prime ministers. More than 700,000

---

44. *Christian Science Monitor,* January 24, 2002; "Pope hosts ecumenical assembly for peace at Assisi," Inq7.net, January 24, 2002.

45. *The Sacramento Bee,* October 16, 2003.

people rubbed shoulders in St. Peter's during the three-hour ceremony. On the streets of Rome, an estimated four million pilgrims watched the funeral through large screens. Around the world, it is estimated that more than two billion people watched the funeral in stadiums, churches, and private homes. It was the largest funeral in the history of the world! And analysts say that it was the largest gathering of world leaders ever!

This remarkable gathering was a rare display of religious plurality and diversity with red-capped Catholic cardinals, black-clad Orthodox priests, Arab head scarves, Jewish scull caps, Central Asian lambskin hats and black veils worn by some women.

And now Pope Benedict XVI, Pope John Paul's most trusted companion, will continue with even sharper voice the strongest statements regarding the importance of Sunday throughout the world. It is largely understood that the new Pope was most probably the writer, or at least the key resource, for much of the heavy literary productions of Pope John Paul II.

In his Christmas message to the world, December 25, 2005, Pope Benedict XVI called for a new world order. He said, "The life-giving power of his light [Christ's] is an incentive for building a *new world order* based on just ethical and economic relationships."[46]

The drum roll doesn't miss a beat!

The new Pontiff argues a concept that Hindus, Buddhists, Muslims, and Christians will have a difficult time objecting to: The Catholic Church is primarily concerned with these "ethical and economic relationships"—these universal moral values based in the nature of man—and the Church will control the meaning of "universal" and "moral." This meaning is wrapped up in how the Church defines "natural law." Finding agreement first in "natural law" (which seems easy today), it is only a half step to Sunday as a day of rest for all in the world—in the interest of the inalienable rights of all mankind.

In speaking to a group of Polish bishops, Pope Benedict XVI

---

46. *ZENIT,* December 25, 2005.

built his case and then said: "It is very important, especially where a pluralistic society prevails, that there be a correct notion of the relationship between the political community and the Church and a clear distinction between the tasks which Christians undertake, individually or as a group, on their own responsibility as citizens guided by the dictates of a Christian conscience, and the activities which, in union with their pastors, they carry out in the name of the Church."[47] Fascinating comment, especially when five Catholic judges are now on the Supreme Court of the United States!

In other words, when the Pope exercises his moral authority, no objective standard outside the Church will be allowed from this point forward to determine what is right and wrong. Catholic politicians, the Pope argues, "must take action against any form of injustice and tyranny, against domination by an individual or a political party and any intolerance."[48] When the Church determines "the nature of the injustice, the tyranny, and the intolerance, no persons or group of persons will be able to assert the claims of the Bible, for instance, as a defense against the claims of the Church." Thus, in the United States, "no appeal to a constitution" will be powerful enough to hold back the encroachments of the Church. Every person in the world will be at the mercy of Rome. There will no earthly power to stop her.[49]

These following, prescient words take on new solemnity today— as if they were written yesterday:

"This is the religion which Protestants are beginning to look upon with so much favor, and which will eventually be united with Protestantism. This union will not, however, be effected by a change in Catholicism, for Rome never changes. She claims infallibility. It is Protestantism that will change. The adoption of liberal ideas on its part will bring it where it can clasp the hand of Catholicism. ... The professed Protestant world will form a confederacy with the man of

---

47. *ZENIT*, December 18, 2005. cited in Marcus Sheffield, http;//www. adventcry.org/archive/2005/12-25-2005.html

48. Ibid.

49. Marcus Sheffield, op. cit.

sin, and the church and the world will be in corrupt harmony."[50]

"And all the world marveled" (Revelation 13:3 NKJV); ("wondered" (KJV)—they "are of one mind" (Revelation 17:13).

---

50. *Last Day Events*, 130.

♦ CHAPTER FOUR ♦

United States—The Great Enabler

For more than 155 years, Sevenh-day Adventist scholars have understood that the study of Revelation 13:11–17 focused on the development and last-day significance of the United States of America.

Of course, more than a century ago, such a line of thought seemed preposterous. But it launched a concept and worldview that has become more relevant today than ever. That the fledgling United States, barely 75 years old, would become a world superpower— well, nothing could have seemed more unimaginable!

John N. Andrews was the first in a long line to spell out the future of the United States. Following his review of history and how major world powers had been predicted in the book of Daniel, Andrews noted that each of the world empires were "ever tending westward" and that following this trend, "we still look westward for the rise of the power described in this prophecy [Revelation 13:11–17]."[1]

Young Andrews did his homework, quoting a current magazine article: "In the west an opposing and still more wonderful American

---

1. *Review and Herald,* May 1851.

empire is E M E R G I N G." In many pages of his 1851 article, John noted the biblical features of this young country that he saw symbolized by the beast with lamb-like horns. For John, these two horns denoted the "civil and religious power of this nation—its Republican civil power, and its Protestant ecclesiastical power."

Later, he observed: "It is of itself a wonder, a system of government which has not its like elsewhere. ... The two-horned beast is from the time of the rise a power contemporary with the first beast [Papacy], and not the first beast in another form." And Andrews goes on to connect the coming showdown between seventh-day Sabbath keepers and those enforcing the "the mark of the beast" through the powers of the two-horned beast, the United States.

Farfetched and Delusional?

This is heady stuff! For those living in the 1850s, this kind of thinking indeed seemed farfetched and delusional. Think about it, the population of this young country was less than 24 million. California, our 31st state, was admitted to the Union only the year before. A 100-acre wheat field remained the largest any one man could farm. In 1850, the first Singer sewing machine was patented. Kerosene and the safety elevator had not yet been invented; a railroad from the East had not yet reached Chicago; and oil had not yet been discovered. Compulsory school attendance was not yet law. And to think that this mostly agricultural expanse would become a world superpower defied credibility!

Why was Andrews so positive about declaring the United States to be the "two-horned" beast of Revelation 13? Obviously, not because of what he read in the newspapers! Young John was reading his Bible! He might also have had access to historical records that had linked the Papacy with the first beast of Revelation 13 for several centuries[2] and the United States with the "two-horned" beast.[3]

---

2. See LeRoy E. Froom, *The Prophetic Faith of Our Fathers*, (Washington, DC: Review and Herald Publishing Association, 1948), vol. 4, 1091, 109.

3. Ibid., 1099.

Now we can understand the validity of another prescient comment written in 1888 regarding the role of the United States as time moved on and as the end-time galloped into the present:

"For about forty years, students of prophecy in the United States have presented this testimony to the world. In the events now taking place is seen a rapid advance toward the fulfillment of the prediction. With Protestant teachers there is the same claim of divine authority for Sunday-keeping, and the same lack of scriptural evidence, as with the papist leaders who fabricated miracles to supply the place of a command from God. The assertion that God's judgments are visited upon men for their violation of the Sunday-sabbath, will be repeated; already it is beginning to be urged. And a movement to enforce Sunday observance is fast gaining ground."[4]

Solemn Days Ahead

But with prophetic insight, Ellen White saw more, ominously more:

▶ "When Protestantism shall stretch her hand across the gulf to grasp the hand of the Roman power, when she shall reach over the abyss to clasp hands with spiritualism, when, under the influence of this threefold union, our country shall repudiate every principle of its Constitution as a Protestant and republican government, and shall make provision for the propagation of papal falsehoods and delusions, then we may know that the time has come for the marvelous working of Satan and that the end is near."[5]

▶ "When the leading churches of the United States, uniting upon such points of doctrine as are held by them in common, shall influence the state to enforce their decrees and to sustain their institutions, then Protestant America will have formed an image of the Roman hierarchy, and the infliction of civil penalties upon dissenters will inevitably result."[6]

---

4. *The Great Controversy*, 579 (1888, 1911).

5. *Testimonies*, vol. 5, 451 (1885).

6. Ibid., 445.

70 NEVER BEEN THIS LATE BEFORE

▶ "The Protestants of the United States will be foremost in stretching their hands across the gulf to grasp the hand of spiritualism; they will reach over the abyss to clasp hands with the Roman power; and under the influence of this threefold union, this country will follow in the steps of Rome in trampling on the rights of conscience."[7]

▶ The beast with two horns is also to say "to them that dwell on the earth, that they should make an image to the beast;" and, furthermore, it is to command all, "both small and great, rich and poor, free and bond" to receive the mark of the beast (Revelation 13:11–16). It has been shown that the United States is the power represented by the beast with lamblike horns, and that this prophecy will be fulfilled when the United States shall enforce Sunday observance, which Rome claims as the special acknowledgment of her supremacy.

▶ "Political corruption is destroying love of justice and regard for truth; and even in free America, rulers and legislators, in order to secure public favor, will yield to the popular demand for a law enforcing Sunday observance. Liberty of conscience, which has cost so great a sacrifice, will no longer be respected. In the soon-coming conflict we shall see exemplified the prophet's words: "The dragon was wroth with the woman, and went to make war with the remnant of her seed, which keep the commandments of God, and have the testimony of Jesus Christ" (Revelation 12:17).[8]

▶ "A time is coming when the law of God is, in a special sense, to be made void in our land. The rulers of our nation will, by legislative enactments, enforce the Sunday law, and thus God's people be brought into great peril. When our nation, in its legislative councils, shall enact laws to bind the consciences of men in regard to their religious privileges, enforcing Sunday observance, and bringing oppressive power to bear against those who keep the seventh-day Sabbath, the law of God will, to all

---

7. Ibid., 588.

8. Ibid., 578, 579, 592.

intents and purposes, be made void in our land; and national apostasy will be followed by national ruin."[9]

▶ "The people of the United States have been a favored people; but when they restrict religious liberty, surrender Protestantism, and give countenance to popery, the measure of their guilt will be full, and "national apostasy" will be registered in the books of heaven. The result of this apostasy will be national ruin."[10]

▶ "As America, the land of religious liberty, shall unite with the papacy in forcing the conscience and compelling men to honor the false sabbath, the people of every country on the globe will be led to follow her example."[11]

▶ "The less we make direct charges against authorities and powers, the greater work we shall be able to accomplish, both America and in foreign countries. Foreign nations will follow the example of the United States. Though she leads out, yet the same crisis will come upon our people in all parts of the world."[12]

Where is this all heading?

What does all this mean? In a quick overview, we note several events that will happen in rapid succession:

▶ Protestants of the United States stretch across the gulf to grasp spiritualism and over the abyss to clasp hands with the Papacy; under this threefold union, this country will follow in the steps of Rome in trampling on the rights of conscience.

▶ Leading churches of the United States unite upon doctrines and/or values held in common, influencing the government to enforce their decrees and to sustain their institutions; thus Protestant America will form an image of the papacy.

▶ Revelation 13 will be fulfilled when the United States enforces

---

9. *Review and Herald,* December 18, 1888.

10. *Review and Herald,* May 2, 1893.

11. *Testimonies,* vol. 6, 18.

12. Ibid., 695

Sunday observance, which Rome claims as the acknowledgment of her supremacy.

▶ Political corruption will destroy love of justice and regard for truth in free America; rulers and legislators, in order to secure public favor, will yield to the popular demand for enforcing Sunday observance. Liberty of conscience will no longer be respected.

▶ Countries all over the earth will follow the example of the United States in exalting the religious leadership of the papacy and in enacting worldwide Sunday laws.

▶ National apostasy is followed by national ruin.

Does any of this sound like someone's delusional conspiracy theory? What do we see in our daily newspapers and round-the-clock TV news? Is there anything farfetched in Ellen White's description of the end time in the United States? Is there anything in her description of the United States in the last days that sounds like a mere projection of what she observed in the 19th century? Does her emphasis on truth—that it should be honored, cherished and protected—sound passé and outmoded in our "progressive," politically correct, and tolerant 21st century?

The uniting of Protestants and Catholics on "common" doctrine

In our last chapter, we noted that in March 1994, 40 prominent religious leaders formulated a document called "Evangelicals and Catholics Together: The Christian Mission in the 3rd Millennium." It could be easily argued that they reversed 500 years of church history. To imply in the document that both sides preach the same Christ, understand authority and the "church" the same way, or hold the same understanding of "justification by grace through faith" is the test of credulity. Yet both sides "contend together" to uphold "sanctity of life, family values, parental choice in education, moral standards in society, and democratic institutions worldwide."

Further, "We affirm that a common set of core values is found in the teachings of religions, and that these form the basis of a global ethic ... and which are the conditions for a sustainable world order." New phrases such as the church being responsible "for the right ordering of civil society" are more than interesting. Further, they agree that "it is neither theologically legitimate nor a prudent use of resources" to proselytize among active members of another Christian community.

Would Martin Luther or any of the other Reformers have said, "Evangelicals and Catholics are brothers and sisters in Christ"?

They affirmed that Evangelicals and Catholics should contend against abortion and pornography and share the common values of honesty, law observance, work, caring, chastity, mutual respect between the sexes, parenthood, and family. And, yes, they contend that "Christians individually and the church corporately also have a responsibility for the right ordering of civil society."

This "right ordering of civil society" fails to distinguish between legislating morality in the area of human freedom and laws that govern how one worships the God of morality. It seems to me that "religious" legislation in the end time will come under the guise of laws that will address social crises—a smooth way to segue into "rational" reasons to unite for the "common good."[13]

Further, as these two religious forces, Evangelicals and Roman Catholics, unite in "common cause" pursuing the "common good," they will prod legislative assembles to "enforce their decrees and to sustain their institutions" which, in essence, is a repeat of papal history, which for centuries would use the state to sustain and

---

13. By executive order on December 12, 2002, President Bush launched his Faith-Based Initiative, a program that promotes federal funding of faith-based organizations. Although funding has been available to religious social service agencies for many years, this executive order permits the giving directly to churches. Gerald Grimaud, former Pennsylvania assistant Attorney General and currently in private practice in Tunkhannock, PA, wrote: "With the breakdown of the wall of separation, both church and state will pay a great price, as will the individual. Yes, church social programs and the needy will benefit in the short run. However, with state funding comes government intrusion into church programs, forms, applications, questions, monitoring, supervising, auditing, managing, and even prosecutions. And over time, sadly, the mission of church programs will be neutered."—*Liberty*, March/April 2003.

enforce its religious programs. This repeat of history is here called "an image of the Roman hierarchy," a mirror reflection of centuries of church-state union—and its appalling consequences.

The result of this civil enforcement of religious decrees will be the "infliction of civil penalties upon dissenters." A national crisis of any kind would make this document of common values a clarion call for all concerned for these common values to rise up in unprecedented national unity—a unity framed in legislation.

Political corruption leads to popular demands

Ellen White forecasted that "political corruption" would destroy "love of justice" and eventually lead to "the popular demand" for the enforcement of a Sunday law. For most people this prediction has seemed absurd—nothing like this could happen in a country that reveres the First Amendment to its Constitution! It all depends on definitions.

For the Supreme Court today to affirm a national Sunday law as a special religious day seems highly unlikely. But the same Court could easily act on precedent and support the contention that Sunday is the most likely day in the week to promote neighborhood and national unity on "common values."

For years, the Supreme Court has used its *Lemon* test to determine church-state relationships. The test opines that a law must have a secular purpose and not advance or hinder the interests of any religion.

But the Supreme Court is not above reversing itself depending on the shifts toward the right or left with replacements. The facts are obvious that religious freedom in the United States is wonderful theory, but the applications of that theory depend on the subjective presuppositions of a vacillating court.

For instance, our constitutional protections were eclipsed after the Japanese attack on Pearl Harbor, December 7, 1941. The imprisonment of approximately 120.000 Americans of Japanese heritage, young and old, proved that in times of national crisis, such protections were nonexistent—all in response to public opinion.

When the Supreme Court upheld Congress and the executive arm, Judge Robert Jackson, in dissent wrote that the ruling was a "subtle blow to liberty. ... The principle then lies like a loaded weapon ready for the hand of any authority that can bring forward a plausible claim of an urgent need."[14]

Omnipotence of the Majority

Alexis de Tocqueville, in his peerless analysis of American life and government, wrote, "If ever the free institutions of America are destroyed, that event may be attributed to the omnipotence of the majority, which may at some future time urge the minorities to desperation."[15]

The day is coming, sooner than most anyone can imagine, when the majority will suddenly look at this country as many foreign countries do today. At a time when our government is trying to sell the American Way of Life worldwide, many countries are doing their best to keep us out. Why? Compared to their cultures, we look decadent and forbidding—they see our crime statistics, our flouting of sexual excess and perversion, our alcohol problems, and the extravagant portrayal of this decadence in our entertainment media.

Any day now the "majority" will sense that the "American Way" of today must return to the "American Way" of a century ago. Revulsion against decadence will become a national issue. The convergence of natural and economic disasters will enflame the general public with a common cry: "Something has to be done!"

The unifying issue that the "majority" will agree on will likely be a national day of rest. Perhaps led by the Evangelicals and Catholics who already have joined hands, "the majority" will demand our legislators, using the language of "urgent need," to force some kind of national unity. In response to the biblical pronouncement that "righteousness exalteth the nation," a national Sunday law would be a visible witness that the United States is pulling its moral house together.

---

14. Korematsu v. United States. 1943.

15. *Democracy in America* (New York, NY: Signet Classic, 2001), 120.

Common Community Day

We are not dealing with future "maybes." In the Netherlands, on December 5, 2002, the *Nederlands Dagblads* reported that two opposing political parties voted to make Sunday a "Community Day" but "their ideas about such a day differ like night and day. The Christian Union asks for the closing of shops on Sundays and strives to make Sunday a day of rest for everyone. By contrast, the Labor Party allows people to do whatever they like on Sundays. ... This law, however, will cut the weekend by 50 percent, from the two days to only one day which will be Sunday, the only official day of rest."

I can assure you that more countries will soon follow—a coming Sunday law in the United States is as real as the sun shining tomorrow morning.

We don't have to look far to see the groundwork already laid for a national Sunday law in the United States. In 1961 a majority ruling of the U. S. Supreme Court in *McGowan v. Maryland* upheld the constitutionality of Sunday laws even though they only happened "to coincide or harmonize" with a religion! Talk about legal fiction! The Court was telling Americans that if the majority were to enjoy the benefits of a uniform day of rest, that benefit would outweigh any burden that such a law would impose on a minority group.

Of course, most anyone could see through that reasoning, *even as the dissenting judges did.* The case would not have come to the Supreme Court if religious underpinnings were not in place! *But the majority ruled.* This 1961 ruling has cast a dark shadow forward; soon thunderclouds will roll.

United States: Superpower

Revelation 13:12–14 outlines an ominous scenario: the United States has the power and influence to lead other nations into "worshiping" the papacy as the spiritual leader of the world. By means of spectacular events, or because of terrible natural disasters, the United States will dramatically grasp the attention of those that "dwell on the earth," linking with the papacy, the linchpin in establishing world peace.

Some might ask, does the United States really have that much world influence and does it really want it?

Incredible as it might have sounded in the 19th century and for most of the 20th, the United States, in a few short years, has been vaulted, by circumstances, into the position of being the only superpower on Planet Earth. No other world power in history— not the Persian nor Roman nor Spanish nor British empires—has ever been the "sole" superpower. Today the United States has no close competitors. America, for example, outspends the next 20 countries combined on its military—a force that the rest of the world expects us to employ as the world's first response to troubles anywhere. But far beyond its military might is America's leadership in technology, economic strength, and humanitarian relief.

Since September 11, 2001, in Afghanistan and Iraq, we've witnessed an unfolding of military capabilities that has astonished the rest of the world. For instance, with a relatively few special ops men, utilizing GPS systems and pilotless planes, the military changed the course of history in a few days in Afghanistan; with the combined capabilities of specially trained men and women, they changed the course of history in Iraq in a few short weeks. Terrorists are being caught, killed, or pursued all over the planet by the most sophisticated gear imaginable.

With the world slipping into common talk regarding the New World Order or global governance (as we saw in the last chapter), the thought that only America could make it happen is a no-brainer.

But what is so incongruous, so difficult to put together, is that the United States, though admittedly the most powerful political nation on earth, is also the foremost example of a nation established on the principles of freedom, both political and religious! The world had never before seen a nation that so resolutely wrapped itself within a phenomenal Declaration of Independence and unparalleled Constitution, such as the first 13 colonies did in 1776 and 1787–9. And then further, in 1791, producing the unprecedented Bill of Rights as the first Ten Amendments to the Constitution.

Both of these unique documents rested on simple principles that were nobly set forth in the Declaration of Independence—"truths to be self-evident, that all men are created equal, and that they are endowed by their Creator with certain unalienable [incapable of being surrendered] rights, among which are life, liberty, and the pursuit of happiness." The document was signed by 56 heroic men under their own personal commitment: "With a firm reliance on the Protection of Divine Providence, we mutually pledge to each other our Lives, our Fortunes and our sacred Honor."

How could this really happen?

So how will Satan's lies and deceptions set the United States up to be the world leader in uniting all nations under a religious authority that has universal clout and enough muscle to enforce economic hardship and persecution on those they hate? How will satanic lies become so believable that "the world worshiped the beast"? (Revelation 13:4).[16]

A Brief Reality Check

In our last chapter, we reviewed Pope John Paul's masterful world strategy. One of his primary goals was to unite the world's religions, especially in his 1994 apostolic letter "Tertio Millennio Adventiente" ("The Coming Third Millennium"). This goal was more directly detailed in his 1995 encyclical "Ut Unum Sin" ("That They May Be One"). And then, among other events in 2000, the U.S. Congress authorized a Congressional Gold Medal to be presented to Pope John Paul II as a recognition of his "preeminent moral authority" and in "transcending temporal politics, has used his moral authority to hasten the fall of godless totalitarian regimes .. has promoted the inner peace of man as well as peace among mankind through his faith-inspired defense of justice, and has thrown open the doors of the Catholic Church, reconciling differences within Christendom as well as reaching out to the world's great religions."

---

16. See chapter seven for a larger examination of evil's four-step strategy that will unfold in its fiercest display in the last of the last days.

Proceeding with his global peace plan, Pope John Paul II gathered more than 100 international religious leaders in Assisi, Italy, in 2002, pursuing "authentic peace."

Pope John Paul II made a point to woo Mecca to Rome. His emphasis that all Christians and Muslims worship the same God, that their mutual responsibility is to build a "civilization of love," is a "logic of love" that will bring all Christians and Muslims together in world peace.

All this is destined to bear fruit. The day is coming when something like the following might happen: Walking across the Hudson River and into the United Nations building, some religious figure (perhaps even a representation of the Virgin Mary) will galvanize world leaders buried under the weight of dozens of world conflicts. From that powerful rostrum, world delegates will hear peace plans to solve Ireland's never-ending hostility between Irish Catholics and Protestants, proposals that will meld Israelis and Palestinians, and do the same for racial divisions in all countries; Muslims and their neighbors the world over will suddenly see a workable plan for peace. The delegates stand in unison, recognizing that this dynamic religious leader has laid out the most sensible solutions for all their problems. They can only wonder why these solutions weren't thought of before! So reasonable, so believable!

The Papacy, working through these political and religious leaders, will soon have its way, breaking down all kinds of traditional international barriers as it receives the adulation of the whole world—an adulation led by the United States. Remember, "All the world marveled and followed the beast. So they worshipped the dragon [Satan] ... who gave authority to the beast; and they [the world] worshipped the beast, saying, 'Who is like the beast?'" Further, the two-horned beast "exercises all the authority of the first beast and causes the earth and those who dwell in it to worship the first beast, whose deadly wound was healed ... and he deceives those who dwell on the earth ... telling those who dwell on the earth to make an image to the beast" (Revelation 12:9; 13:3, 4, 11–14).

Almost in contrapuntal fugue relationship, religious leaders in the United States are unfolding the predictions of Revelation 13. Religious leaders throughout the nation focused on "Ten Commandments Day," Sunday, May 7, 2006. Tens of thousands of congregations across the United States heard their pastor emphasize the importance and authority of God's law. Hard to imagine! Strange as it may seem, Protestant and Jewish stalwarts are increasingly united in support of the Ten Commandments' relevancy—a posture that is 180 degrees from most of their rhetoric for more than a century. Unfortunately, however, they are not yielding to the obvious intent of the fourth commandment.

What is their driving purpose? They point to a host of disturbing trends and court actions that "have threatened the very fabric and foundation of our culture and faith. The Ten Commandments and all other references to God, which have served as the moral foundation and anchor of our great country, are systematically being removed from public places. Public displays of the Ten Commandments and other symbols of our faith have been a powerful visual testimony to the fact that the United States of America is 'one nation under God.' Their removal from public places shows that those with a secular humanist agenda are intent on destroying the moral heritage of our nation. ...The Ten Commandment Commission was founded to counter the secular agenda and help restore the Ten Commandments and Judeo-Christian values to their rightful place in our society."[17]

In his book, *The New World Order*, Pat Robertson writes:

"The utopians have talked of world order. Without saying so explicitly, the Ten Commandments set the only order that will bring world peace—with devotion to and respect of God at the center, strong family bonds and respect next, and the sanctity of people, property, family, reputation, and peace of mind next."[18]

In respect to the fourth commandment, the Sabbath, Robertson wrote:

---

17. Website for the Ten Commandment Commission: http://tencommandmentsday.com/home.html

18. *The New World Order* (Dallas: Word Publishing, 1991), 233.

"The next obligation that a citizen of God's world order owes is to himself. 'Remember the Sabbath day, to keep it holy,' is a command for the personal benefit of each citizen. Our minds, spirits, and bodies demand a regular time of rest. Perhaps God's greatest gift to mankind's earthly existence is the ability to be free from work one day a week."[19]

Pat Robinson is only one voice among many who are calling for the necessity and urgency of Sunday sacredness. From labor union leaders, official denominational resolutions, magazine columnists, and the papacy itself, the crescendo is developing. Note Pope John Paul II's (July 7, 1998) apostolic letter *Dies Domini (The Lord's Day).*[20]

Worldwide Polarization Against Sabbath-keepers

What seems most incredible at the moment is the prediction that there will be a *worldwide* polarization against Sabbath-keepers.

---

19. Ibid., 236.

20. See last chapter for more elaboration of this apostolic letter: "62. It is the duty of Christians therefore to remember that, although the practices of the Jewish Sabbath are gone, surpassed as they are by the 'fulfillment' which Sunday brings, the underlying reasons for keeping 'the Lord's Day' holy— inscribed solemnly in the Ten Commandments—remain valid, though they need to be reinterpreted in the light of the theology and spirituality of Sunday. ... 64. For several centuries, Christians observed Sunday simply as a day of worship, without being able to give it the specific meaning of Sabbath rest. Only in the fourth century did the civil law of the Roman Empire recognize the weekly recurrence, determining that on 'the day of the sun' the judges, the people of the cities and the various trade corporations would not work. ... 65. By contrast, the link between the Lord's Day and the day of rest in civil society has a meaning and importance, which go beyond the distinctly Christian point of view. The alternation between work and rest, built into human nature, is willed be God himself, as appears in the creation story in the Book of Genesis. ... In this matter, my predecessor Pope Leo XIII in his Encyclical *Rerum Novarum* speaks of Sunday rest as a worker's right which the State must guarantee. In our own historical context there remains the obligations to ensure that everyone can enjoy the freedom, rest and relaxation which human dignity requires, together with the associated religious, family, cultural and interpersonal needs which are difficult to meet if there is no guarantee of at least one day of the week on which people can *both* rest and celebrate. ... 67. ... Therefore, also in the particular circumstances of our own time, Christians will naturally strive to ensure that civil legislation respects their duty to keep Sunday holy."—*Dies Domini,* July 7, 1998.

The universal authority of the "beast" power of Revelation 13 will, with great craft, use the panic being caused throughout the world by natural disasters, interlocking economic distress, and unsettled ethnic/religious conflicts to accomplish its long-sought goals. The prestige and power of the United States will become the model of how to unify the majority around the world in calling for God to calm the world's storms as surely as Jesus calmed the raging Sea of Galilee.

It almost takes one's breath away: when "America, the land of religious liberty, shall unite with the papacy in forcing the conscience and compelling men to honor the false sabbath, the people of every country on the globe will be led to follow her example."[21] "The Sabbath question is to be the issue in the great final conflict in which all the world will act a part."[22] A "new world order," indeed!

All of these predictions regarding the impact of a politico-religio virus (such as the international enforcement of Sunday laws) that begins like a pimple in the United States but one day will spread rapidly through the blood stream of world communities is no longer a bad dream. Most dialogue on almost any TV talk show or weekly magazine refers to the worldwide influence and power of the United States. When the United States selects the foreign countries that will receive billions of dollars annually on the basis of what's best for America, when terrible earthquakes and famines call forth massive U.S. humanitarian relief anywhere in the world, when the nations of the world expect the U. S. military to resolve civil wars overseas, no one any more doubts the clout of American opinion and action.

Since September 11, 2001, the ability of U.S. might to remain a benign banker to the world morphed into the realization that something must be done to guarantee peace, prosperity, and the spread of human rights on every continent. Such goals in order to survive "will require the expenditure of American will and might." Condoleezza Rice, National Security Adviser to President George

---

21. *Last Day Events*, 135.

22. Ibid.

W. Bush, when asked if the United States is "overly ambitious," replied: "Was it overly ambitious of the United States to believe that democracy could be fostered in Japan and that peace could finally be brought between Germany and France? It succeeded because it proceeded from values that Americans understand. Truman and his team understood that America could not afford to leave a vacuum in the world."[23]

Last Act in the Drama

A significant time factor kicks in at this point—the actual enforcement of Sunday laws worldwide becomes "the last act in the drama. When this enforcement becomes universal God will reveal Himself. When the laws of men are exalted above the laws of God, when the powers of this earth try to force men to keep the first day of the week, know that the time has come for God to work."[24]

Obviously this is almost too much to contemplate at this time. Adventists are known the world over as law-abiding people. In addition, they are also known for their unambiguous defense of America's liberties, even willing to die for them when their president calls for their services in time of war.

But because of world panic and the crafty manipulation of legislators and jurists, "the whole world is to be stirred with enmity against Seventh-day Adventists."[25] And the *pseudo-logic* will prevail:

"The whole world keeps Sunday, they say, and why should not this people, who are so few in number, do according to the laws of the land?"[26] "The judges will refuse to listen to the reasons of those who are loyal to the commandments of God because they know the arguments in favor of the fourth commandment are unanswerable.

---

23. Jay Tolson, "The New American Empire?" *U.S. News & World Report*, January 13, 2003.

24. *Last Day Events*, 135.

25. Ibid., 136.

26. Ibid.

They will say, 'We have a law, and by our law he ought to die.' God's law is nothing to them. 'Our law' with them is supreme. Those who respect this human law will be favored, but those who will not bow to the idol sabbath have no favors shown them."[27]

Adventists in many levels of government and in the academic and business world will discover that their friends of "wealth, genius, [and] education, will combine to cover them with contempt. Persecuting rulers, ministers, and church members will conspire against them. With voice and pen, by boasts, threats, and ridicule, they will seek to overthrow their faith ... [they] shall be treated as traitors ... denounced as enemies of law and order, as breaking down the moral restraints of society, causing anarchy and corruption. ... Their conscientious scruples will be pronounced obstinacy, stubbornness, and contempt of authority."[28]

Word Games

Of course, governments must balance liberty of the individual with security of the individual. The problem is that word games are often played such as "anti-terrorism" or "child protection" and "common values." Such words can easily attack the constitutional rights of the proposed "enemy."

Well-intentioned prosecutors and courts can easily mask and override, in the name of freedom, fundamental rights such as preventive detention, denial of detainee's rights to counsel, the right to prepare a defense, to interview and call witnesses, the right to trial and due process before sentencing, etc. These are basic rights for which tens of thousands of American service men have fought and died.

If every there was a time for mental and moral clarity in the Adventist Church, it is now! It is now time for Adventist lawyers and judges to speak out in defense of the God-given right of individual freedom when it comes to conscience and core beliefs. It is now time for church leadership, including pastors and

---

27. Ibid., 145.

28. Ibid., 146.

administrators, to think boldly regarding their responsibility to lead their church into careful thinking—before the storm breaks! Emotional identification with euphemistic words snared Germany under Hitler, including many Adventist leaders.

A Powerful Heads-up

We are not talking in general terms, nor in the complacency that it will not happen "in my day." Nor should we think that the potential confusion would come from some other group than one's own! We should all contemplate in great seriousness the following prediction, a prediction just as certain as the coming of Jesus:

"As the storm approaches, a large class who have professed faith in the third angel's message, but have not been sanctified through obedience to the truth, abandon their position and join the ranks of the opposition. By uniting with the world and partaking of its spirit, they have come to view matters in nearly the same light; and when the test is brought, they are prepared to choose the easy, popular side. Men of talent and pleasing address, who once rejoiced in the truth, employ their powers to deceive and mislead souls. They become the bitterest enemies of their former brethren. When Sabbathkeepers are brought before the courts to answer for their faith, these apostates are the most efficient agents of Satan to misrepresent and accuse them, and by false reports and insinuations to stir up the rulers against them."[29]

If this preview of things to come is not a powerful heads-up, then I don't know what can get our attention.

In her chapter entitled "The Impending Conflict,"[30] Ellen White provided the background for the amazing shift from post-modernism (wherein authority is abandoned and personal feeling/opinion are the norms) to the time when "reasons" are given for the enforcement of laws that deny others the right of religious liberty. (We have seen many examples that have taken place in the last 40 years.):

---

29. *The Great Controversy*, 608.

30. Ibid., 582-592.

"And as the claims of the fourth commandment are urged upon the people, it is found that the observance of the seventh-day Sabbath is enjoined; and as the only way to free themselves from a duty which they are unwilling to perform, popular teachers declare that the law of God is no longer binding. Thus they cast away the law and the Sabbath together. As the work of Sabbath reform extends, this rejection of the divine law to avoid the claims of the fourth commandment will become well-nigh universal. The teachings of religious leaders have opened the door to infidelity, to Spiritualism, and to contempt for God's holy law, and upon these leaders rests a fearful responsibility for the iniquity that exists in the Christian world.

"Yet this very class put forth the claim that the fast-spreading corruption is largely attributable to the desecration of the so-called "Christian Sabbath," and that the enforcement of Sunday observance would greatly improve the morals of society."[31]

After her predictions of end-time disasters of all kinds and that "these visitations are to become more and more frequent and disastrous," she wrote:

"And then the great deceiver will persuade men that those who serve God are causing these evils. The class that have provoked the displeasure of Heaven will charge all their troubles upon those whose obedience to God's commandments is a perpetual reproof to transgressors. It will be declared that men are offending God by the violation of the Sunday-sabbath, that this sin has brought calamities which will not cease until Sunday observance shall be strictly enforced, and that those who present the claims of the fourth commandment, thus destroying reverence for Sunday, are troublers of the people, preventing their restoration to divine favor and temporal prosperity."[32]

Even more explicit, Mrs. White previewed how those proclaiming the legitimacy of the seventh day of the week as the biblical Sabbath will be declared "lawbreakers":[33]

---

31. Ibid., 587.

32. Ibid., 590.

33. Ibid., 591.

"Those who honor the Bible Sabbath will be denounced as enemies of law and order, as breaking down the moral restraints of society, causing anarchy and corruption, and calling down the judgments of God upon the earth. Their conscientious scruples will be pronounced obstinacy, stubbornness, and contempt of authority. ... Ministers who deny the obligation of the divine law will present from the pulpit the duty of yielding obedience to the civil authorities as ordained of God. In legislative halls and courts of justice, commandment-keepers will be misrepresented and condemned. A false coloring will be given to their words; the worst construction will be put upon their motives."[34]

Such unambiguous forecasts were only a 19th outline of the future in the United States and the rest of the world. Here in the beginning of the 21st century, we are living in the enormous and spectacular unfolding of these predicted insights:

▶ Protestant spokesmen declare that God's law is no longer binding and that the seventh-day Sabbath was a Jewish custom—thus removing the religious argument for the authority of the fourth commandment of the Decalogue.

▶ At the same time, others will declare that calamities are the result of God's displeasure on those who are "violating" the Sunday sabbath.

▶ The rise of end-time corruption becomes one of the reasons for supporting Sunday sacredness and regaining temporal prosperity. Joining the "corruption" argument will be the colossal increase and severity of natural disasters—further "reasons" for national action to show God our collective repentance.

▶ When supporters of the seventh-day Sabbath continue their defense of religious liberty and the biblical Sabbath, they will be "denounced as enemies of law and order"—an amazing, illogical charge.

▶ In the halls of justice, supporters of the biblical Sabbath will be "misrepresented and condemned." "A false coloring" will be given to their defense of freedom and biblical authority.

34. Ibid., 592.

No one today can accurately imagine how all this will play out. We can only guess at the specific national crises that will generate a call for national unity of those who will vote for common values in the hope that God can bring peace to the nation. All the while, this surge for national unity leading to Sunday enforcement will bring out the worst in people who prefer legislation rather than dialogue over the issues that divide.

The various crises will feed on each other, whether they are economic, terrorism, rampant disease, or natural disasters. It will only spell "national ruin" and the prelude to the seven last plagues. Probation will close. The neural pathways of faithful loyalists who regard the commandments of God as their hedge and joy are settled into the truth so that they will never, ever, say no to God. The neural pathways of those who have rejected the wooing of the Holy Spirit are also settled into a pattern of self-will and absorption. They too will never change—habit patterns are set forever.[35]

What should we conclude in this review of United States in prophecy?

That which might have seemed farfetched in the middle of the 19th century is front-page news today. Although the world influence of the papacy and the United States was many years in the future, biblical scholars such as John N. Andrews painted an amazing scenario of the future, on the basis of biblical study alone. Ellen White emphatically enlarged this biblical picture in ways that no one on earth could have imagined in her day—but how precisely her predictions have become daily reality!

Adventists don't get their prophetical understanding from reading today's news. Never have, and never will. They let the newsmakers validate their prophetical road map, not write it. In other words, we don't recreate our view of last-day events in every

---

35. "Just as soon as the people of God are sealed in their foreheads—it is not any seal or mark that can be seen but a settling into the truth, both intellectually and spiritually, so they cannot be moved—just as soon as God's people are sealed and prepared for the shaking, it will come. Indeed, it has begun already." *Last Day Events*, 219, 220.

new generation. We "have the prophetic word made more sure" (2 Peter 1:19, NKJV).

Adventists in the 19th century may have had to use their imagination. Adventists today only have to use their eyes and ears. Nightfall does not come at once. At twilight, everything remains seemingly unchanged. But at twilight we should sense the coolness of the air, lest we suddenly become victims of the darkness.[36]

God never leaves His people without "present truth" (2 Peter 1:12). Why did God give this picture of the future to Ellen White? Because He has never left His people without "present truth." John the Revelator wrote that in the end time, the Papacy's "deadly wound was healed" (Revelation 13:13). That time has come! Much beyond anyone's anticipation even 40 years ago! It surely is "present truth" today.

Ellen White offers end-time people clear, believable counsel:

"In order to endure the trial before them, they must understand the will of God as revealed in his Word; they can honor him only as they have a right conception of his character, government, and purposes, and act in accordance with them. None but those who have fortified the mind with the truths of the Bible will stand through the last great conflict."[37]

Our response to God's graciousness and the counsel of His last-day messenger is to keep walking into the light until the Light bearer returns. Everyone in the world has enough light to make moral decisions, even though it might be only a crack in the door.

No other people have a clearer map for the road ahead. No other people have been given the responsibility of sharing the truth about the future with others. How will we ever face up to reality when we realize that we knew something about the future that we could have

---

36. Thoughts that I remember Supreme Court Justice William O. Douglas saying, although I can't remember the words exactly. The truth he is emphasizing will be never more needed than in the days ahead.

37. *The Great Controversy*, p. 593.

made clearer to our children, to our neighbors, to men and women everywhere—but we neglected this privilege and duty?

The only peaceful, reassuring way to face the last of the last days is to keep trusting God's Word, which alone can give us the road map.

♦ CHAPTER FIVE ♦

When We Can't Always Believe Our Eyes or Ears

Something happened in 1848 that would dramatically change the appeal of Spiritualism (or Spiritism[1])—a thrust that would unfold beyond anyone's imagination in the mid–19th century—an unfolding that would have profound implications in the end time.

Historians generally agree that the modern spiritualist movement began with the "knocking" or "rapping" on the walls of a home in Hydesville, New York, about 35 miles east of Rochester, the home of the Fox family. This unexpected development was far different than the odd behavior of other self-styled spiritualizers.

---

1. "Spiritism is the name properly given to the belief that the living can and do communicate with the spirits of the departed, and to the various practices by which such communication is attempted. It should be carefully distinguished from *Spiritualism*, the philosophical doctrine which holds, in general, that there is a spiritual order of beings no less real than the material and, in particular, that the soul of man is a spiritual substance. Spiritism, moreover ... seeks to establish a world-wide religion in which the adherents of the various traditional faiths, setting their dogmas aside, can unite."— *Catholic Encyclopedia*, www.newadvent.org/cathen/1422`a.htm

91

No longer closeted in darkened rooms bathed in candlelight, followers holding hands, etc., prominent men and women now emerged as advocates by pen and practice.

What is behind all this? The common assumption underlying this widespread interest in modern-day Spiritualism is the notion of the "immortal soul," advocated by both Catholics and most Protestants. Without that false belief, Spiritualism would not exist today. Probably not one in a million today realize that this notion entered the Christian church, not from biblical teachings, but straight out of Grecian philosophy. But that is a topic for another book!

Hydesville, New York

Back to Hydesville, New York, on March 31, 1848, where Kate and Margaret Fox reported that they were frightened by the strange tapping or knocking on a wall, by bedclothes being pulled off the bed, and furniture moved around the room. After controlling their fears, they devised a code system by which they could communicate with the "knocker." Further research indicated that the sisters were communicating with the departed murdered spirit of Charles B. Rosna, killed in that home. And modern spiritualism, "talking" with evil spirits, was born![2] What was extraordinary about this report was "the spirit" communicated through these physical "rappings," and not simply through a person in a trance.

For 60 years, the writings of Emanuel Swedenborg and the teachings of Franz Mesmer provided the basis for those seeking personal knowledge of the afterlife. Swedenborg believed he could, in a trance state, "commune" with spirits and his writings described the spirit world. Proclaiming that there is no heaven or hell, but rather a series of spheres through which the "departed spirit" ascended into higher levels of wisdom, he taught that these "spirits" could mediate between God and humans.[3]

2. The two went on tour, promoting spiritualism. Other people joined them as mediums. In 1853, the first Spiritualist Church was founded and within two years, claimed to have two million followers.

3. Followers of Swedenborg have organized under the name "Church of New Jerusalem."

Mesmer did not deal in religious beliefs, but he introduced a technique, later called mesmerism (often, hypnotism), that could induce trances, in which the living could contact departed loved ones or spiritual beings in general.

These two streams of thought (Swedenborgianism and Mesmerism) combined in a strange American synthesis of modern Spiritualism. Interesting, this new thought movement provided one of the first forums for American women to speak to mixed audiences. Radical Quakers, campaigning for abolition and equal rights for women, helped put a "reform" stamp on the young movement.

As one would guess, all this led to widespread fraud, leading to independent investigating commissions that repeatedly established the fraud verdict. Nevertheless, something about Spiritualism was attractive to not only the general public, but also for a growing list of American scientists and authors, and even the Sherlock Holmes creator, Arthur Conan Doyle. Doyle contended that the constant focus on actual observation of phenomena kept English and American Spiritualists from embracing the eastern emphasis on reincarnation. Doyle is often called the "St. Paul" of modern Spiritualism.

Though disorganized, the movement spread throughout the world, but only in the United Kingdom did it become as popular as in the United States. Brazil blended spiritualistic principles with religion (called Spiritism) with millions of followers today. American Spiritualists would meet in private homes for séances, at lecture halls for trance lectures, at summer camps by the thousands—but it remained individualistic. In fact, for many years, medium and trance lecturers resisted any organization attempts!

Two Forms

The movement takes two forms: 1) physical phenomena, usually in private séances by means of raps, audible voices, or most often, materialized figures of departed loved ones; 2) mental phenomena through the mind of a medium by clairvoyance (medium "hears" the spirit) or clairsentience (the medium senses the presence and thought of someone in the room).

Most Spiritists attend Christian churches. Within the Christian environment, Spiritists accept the same moral system, a belief in the Judeo-Christian God, mystical panentheism, Sunday services, and the singing of hymns.

Along with these similarities, Spiritualists and Spiritists do not believe that acts in this life lead the departed "spirit" into an eternity of heaven or hell, but into those constantly ascending spheres. Although they accept most biblical principles, they do not believe that the Bible is the primary source of knowledge, either about God or the afterlife.[4] Further, they believe that death is not a result of sin but part of the divine purpose.

In the latter half of the 20th century, Spiritualism became increasingly syncretic (that is, embracing various forms of the New Age movement). In fact, there is much less interest in miraculous "materializing" mediumship—the kind that captivated Arthur Conan Doyle. Modern Spiritualists prefer the term "Survivalism." A wide audience watches their television channel, called the *Psychic Friends Network*.[5]

A few months after this phenomenon was hitting the news in 1848, a young religious visionary wrote at Topsham, Maine, March 24, 1849:

"I saw that the mysterious knocking in New York and other places was the power of Satan, and that such things would be more and more common, clothed in a religious garb so as to lull the deceived to greater security and to draw the minds of God's

---

4. "Universal Spiritualism is the Science, Philosophy and Religion of continuous life, based upon the demonstrated fact of communication, by means of spiritual channeling, with those who are in the spiritual world."— http://home.comcast.net/~spiritualism/Main/Main.html

5. For many today, Spiritualism is "scientific proof" of life after death, which didn't involve any of the so-called nonsense of religion. In recent years, New Thought Spiritualism seeks to promote the original intent of Spiritualism that has been lost due to the focus on spirit communication over the development of spirituality. The existence of any power or presence opposed to Infinite Intelligence is denied. Evil and suffering are caused by man's ignorance. New Thought Spiritualism does not have any creed; everyone has the right to his own beliefs. Everyone is a potential mystic and spirit communication is a tool to help us understand the true nature of the universe and to help all to develop to the highest possible extent.

people, if possible, to those things and cause them to doubt the teachings and power of the Holy Ghost."[6]

"The mysterious rapping with which modern Spiritualism began was not the result of human trickery or cunning, but was the direct work of evil angels, who thus introduced one of the most successful of soul-destroying delusions. Many will be ensnared through the belief that Spiritualism is a merely human imposture; when brought face to face with manifestations which they cannot but regard as supernatural, they will be deceived, and will be led to accept them as the great power of God."[7]

Evil Angels

Here we learned early on that the "mysterious rapping" was not mysterious, but rather the work of evil angels, although perceived by many as the power of God; the phenomenon would fast spread beyond the Fox sisters who now worked in traveling circuses and local vaudevilles.

And spread it did. Rapidly it was accepted in the Protestant and Catholic world because they had no doctrinal buffer to protect those beguiled by the undeniable manifestations of "mysterious" powers. Three major spiritualist churches exist today: the International General Assembly of Spiritualists, the National Spiritual Alliance of the U.S.A., and the National Spiritualist Association of Churches. Encyclopedias cover spiritualism as a religion—just as Ellen White, the early visionary, predicted even though in her day not much evidence for this remarkable growth existed.

New Age Beliefs

Part of the amazing advance of New Age thought and practice in the last half of the 20th century rests on its claim to communicate with the dead. Channeling is one of its best-known features. Mesmerism, or better known today as certain forms of

---

6. *Review and Herald*, August 1, 1849.

7. *The Great Controversy*, 553.

Hypnotism, is a well-known element of Spiritualistic philosophy; Swedenborg practiced bringing back messages from other spirits, along with Mesmer and Stefan Zweig. They believed that such powers added to the healing art—calling it "spirit healing by the entranced medium."

In recent years, Spiritualism has contributed much to the New Age phenomenon. The New Age movement is a vague term for a collection of ideas derived from both Eastern and Western religious traditions and paganism. Common to all is the belief that spirituality is very individual and that all people are, in some way, divine. Many New Agers believe in spiritual healing, channeling, ESP, dream interpretation, and many other psychic phenomena, developing spirituality by contacting spirits or getting in touch with one's past lives.

Ellen White received her second vision on modern spiritualism on March 24, 1849, and described it on August 24, 1850:

"I saw that the 'mysterious rapping' was the power of Satan; some of it was directly from him, and some indirectly, through his agents, but it all proceeded from Satan. It was his work that he accomplished in different ways; yet many in the churches and the world were so enveloped in gross darkness that they thought and held forth that it was the power of God. Said the angel, 'Should not a people seek unto their God? for the living to the dead?' Should the living go to the dead for knowledge? The dead know not anything. For the living God do ye go to the dead? They have departed from the living God to converse with the dead who know not anything.' See Isaiah 8:19, 20.

"I saw that soon it would be considered blasphemy to speak against the rapping, and that it would spread more and more, that Satan's power would increase, and some of his devoted followers would have power to work miracles, and even to bring down fire from heaven in the sight of men. I was shown that by the rapping and mesmerism, these modern magicians would yet account for all the miracles wrought by our Lord Jesus Christ, and that many would believe that all the mighty works of the Son of God when on earth were accomplished by this same power.

"I was pointed back to the time of Moses, and saw the signs and wonders which God wrought through him before Pharaoh, most of which were imitated by the magicians of Egypt; and that just before the final deliverance of the saints, God would work powerfully for His people, and these modern magicians would be permitted to imitate the work of God."[8]

Blasphemy?

I find these clear, unambiguous words to be astonishing, remembering that they were written when followers of Spiritualism were exceedingly few. Here Ellen White predicted that the time would come when those who opposed Spiritualism will be accused of "blasphemy."

It will not surprise me when governments, in most western countries to begin with, will make it a criminal act to speak against Spiritualists. Laws are already on the books forbidding disparagement against anyone's ethnicity, sexual gender, and religious beliefs. Canadian judges, as I write, are already implementing these laws against those who are only voicing their right to express their own religious beliefs. In the politically correct society, we may be only a half-step away from being jailed for speaking against Spiritualism.

Note one of their own declarations found in their 1948 *Centennial Book of Modern Spiritualism:* "Neither priest nor press should uncharitably speak of, or touch this holy word Spiritualism, only with clean hands and pure hearts, and Spiritualists themselves should honor their blessed gospel of immortality."

Mrs. White predicted that specialists in extrasensory perception would recognize that these "mysterious powers" were far beyond humanly devised tricks of a master magician. "Satan's power would increase" and some of "his followers would have power to work miracles"—experiments in many extrasensory perceptions validate that something beyond human explanation is happening.

In the *Encyclopedia Americana*, the founder of Duke University's Institute for Parapsychology wrote, "The question raised by

---

8. *Early Writings*, 59.

Spiritualism must be faced as one of science's greatest problems."

Two Other Aspects

This vision of 1850 zeroed in on two other aspects that then seemed incredible. The time would come, Ellen White said, when theologians and others would credit Christ's miracles to the powers of Spiritualism. How accurate she was!

The second aspect was that in the last of the last days, "God would work powerfully for His people, and these modern magicians [Spiritualists] would be permitted to imitate the work of God."[9] Compare Revelation 13:13, 14.

In 1854, Mrs. White elaborated on the counsel she had previously given regarding the rise of Spiritualism:

> "I saw the rapping delusion—what progress it was making, and that if it were possible it would deceive the very elect. Satan will have power to bring before us the appearance of forms purporting to be our relatives or friends now sleeping in Jesus. It will be made to appear as if these friends were present; the words that they uttered while here, with which we were familiar, will be spoken, and the same tone of voice that they had while living will fall upon the ear. All this is to deceive the saints and ensnare them into the belief of this delusion."[10]

Loved Ones Appear

Here was added counsel to an emerging Adventist movement with a last-day assignment. Think, would it not be hard to think of a more subtle temptation—to have your "loved one" re–appear, talking about matters that only the departed and you could possibly know? And then for the "loved one" to contradict such plain Bible truths as the atonement, the state of the dead, etc.?

Ellen White gave us clear instruction as to how to repel Satan's master plans to deceive the world in the end time:

9. *Early Writings*, 60.

10. Ibid., 87.

"I saw that the saints must get a thorough understanding of present truth, which they will be obliged to maintain from the Scriptures. They must understand the state of the dead; for the spirits of devils will yet appear to them, professing to be beloved friends and relatives, who will declare to them that the Sabbath has been changed, also other unscriptural doctrines. They will do all in their power to excite sympathy and will work miracles before them to confirm what they declare. The people of God must be prepared to withstand these spirits with the Bible truth that the dead know not anything, and that they who appear to them are the spirits of devils. Our minds must not be taken up with things around us, but must be occupied with the present truth and a preparation to give a reason of our hope with meekness and fear."[11]

Then Ellen White pictured a parable that has never left my mind since reading it more than 60 years ago. I don't think you will ever forget it either:

"I saw the rapidity with which this delusion was spreading. A train of cars was shown me, going with the speed of lightning. The angel bade me look carefully. I fixed my eyes upon the train. It seemed that the whole world was on board, that there could not be one left. Said the angel, 'They are binding in bundles ready to burn.' Then he showed me the conductor, who appeared like a stately, fair person, whom all the passengers looked up to and reverenced. I was perplexed and asked my attending angel who it was. He said, 'It is Satan. He is the conductor in the form of an angel of light. He has taken the world captive. They are given over to strong delusions, to believe a lie, that they may be damned. This agent, the next highest in order to him, is the engineer, and other of his agents are employed in different offices as he may need them, and they are all going with lightning speed to perdition.'"

The rest of these pages in *Early Writings*, pages 87–91, contain additional counsel that you will not read anywhere else.

---

11. Ibid.

Modern Spiritualism Everywhere

Wherever we look today, we are awash in various forms of Spiritualism, from the magazines at checkout stands in the local grocery store to TV programs such as the January 1987, five-hour program, wherein the American Broadcasting Company featured actress Shirley MacLaine's "personal trek through a psychic world." Amazing!

Everywhere we look, we find more examples of Ellen White's vision-based predictions.[12] As I write, Allison DuBois, author of *Don't Kiss Them Good-bye* and her recently released *We Are Their Heaven*, is also famous for inspiring the NBC series, "Medium," starring Emmy-winning actress Patricia Arquette. Her story was featured in a two-page spread in the *Sacramento Bee*—a most remarkable recital of her lifelong connection with the dead. She has been tested by specialists in psychic phenomena, trying to prove to herself that her experiences were not purely subjective and without convincing evidence. The scientists' jaws dropped![13]

Another feature of the last few decades is the astounding fantasy game "Dungeons and Dragons." But this attraction has morphed into even more sophisticated and cruel games such as RuneQuest, Chivalry & Sorcery, Arduin Grimoire, Tunnells and Trolls, etc. Called "Fantasy Role Playing (FRP)," the players, mostly the young, identify with the characters, either good or bad. These games have been called the most magnificently packaged introduction to the occult in recorded history.[14]

Another phenomenon of the last 50 years has been the growing awareness in the medical community of the importance of the "spiritual," that the whole person needs treatment, not just the illness. Ellen White emphasized this spiritual component in much of her writings, especially in *The Ministry of Healing*.

---

12. Think of the Harry Potter phenomenon. Or Marshall Applewhite, founder of the Heaven's Gate cult, whose 39 members committed mass suicide in March 1997, believing they'd ascend to a spaceship hiding in the trail of the comet Hale-Bopp. They were inspired by *Star Wars*.

13. *The Sacramento Bee*, June 19, 2006.

14. Gary North, *None Dare Call it Witchcraft*.

But along with the good comes the counterfeit. Enter the Spiritualist Healer, one who, either through his or her own "inborn power" or through mediumship, is able to transmit curative energies to physical conditions. The results of Spiritual Healing are produced in several ways: 1) By spiritual influences working through the body of the medium to transmit curative energies to the diseased parts of the recipient's body; 2) By spiritual influences enlightening the mind of the medium so that the cause, nature, and seat of the disease in the recipient is made known to the medium. The wide interest in TV healing by certain charismatic preachers dovetails in with modern Spiritualism.

In her book *The Great Controversy*, Ellen White included a chapter on "Spiritualism," ending with this forecast:

> "Little by little he has prepared the way for his master-piece of deception in the development of Spiritualism. He has not yet reached the full accomplishment of his designs; but it will be reached in the last remnant of time. Says the prophet: 'I saw three unclean spirits like frogs. ... They are the spirits of devils, working miracles, which go forth unto the kings of the earth and of the whole world, to gather them to the battle of that great day of God Almighty' (Revelation 16:13, 14)."[15]

World Impact

In these few words, we are looking at the final crescendo of the tsunami wave begun in Hydesville, New York, in 1849. The world impact of Spiritualism cannot even at this late date be fully imagined! Let us follow Ellen White's vision-forecast of the end times. Note the international impact of Spiritualism:

> "Fearful sights of a supernatural character will soon be revealed in the heavens, in token of the power of miracle-working demons. The spirits of devils will go forth to the kings of the earth and to the whole world, to fasten them in deception, and urge them on to unite with Satan in his last struggle against the government of heaven. By these agencies, rulers and subjects will be alike deceived. Persons will arise pretending to be Christ Himself, and claiming the title and

---

15. *The Great Controversy*, 561, 562.

worship, which belong to the world's Redeemer. They will perform wonderful miracles of healing and will profess to have revelations from heaven contradicting the testimony of the Scriptures."[16]

Not only will Spiritualism be a uniting, cohesive manipulator in end-time politics. The master Spiritualist will personally enter the horrendous confusion that he, himself, has sponsored:

"As the crowning act in the great drama of deception, Satan himself will personate Christ. The church has long professed to look to the Saviour's advent as the consummation of her hopes. Now the great deceiver will make it appear that Christ has come. In different parts of the earth, Satan will manifest himself among men as a majestic being of dazzling brightness, resembling the description of the Son of God given by John in the Revelation. Revelation 1:13–15. The glory that surrounds him is unsurpassed by anything that mortal eyes have yet beheld. The shout of triumph rings out upon the air: 'Christ has come! Christ has come!' The people prostrate themselves in adoration before him, while he lifts up his hands and pronounces a blessing upon them, as Christ blessed His disciples when He was upon the earth. His voice is soft and subdued, yet full of melody. In gentle, compassionate tones he presents some of the same gracious, heavenly truths that the Saviour uttered; he heals the diseases of the people, and then, in his assumed character of Christ, he claims to have changed the Sabbath to Sunday, and commands all to hallow the day, which he has blessed. He declares that those who persist in keeping holy the seventh day are blaspheming his name by refusing to listen to his angels sent to them with light and truth. This is the strong, almost overmastering delusion. ...

"But the people of God will not be misled. The teachings of this false christ are not in accordance with the Scriptures."[17]

God's early warning system from 1849 through the 1880s sounded like a wild dream, a neurotic fantasy to those first reading or hearing these predictions. But we today have seen how rapidly "mysterious rappings" became a worldwide phenomenon. Once

---

16. Ibid.,, 624.

17. Ibid.,, 624.

considered an object of interest in vaudeville, Spiritualism soon became baptized, taking its place among Christian denominations. Chief among its "miracles" would be the "return" of dead loved ones, proving to many that Spiritualism was more than magic. This immortality of the soul notion is reflected in such activities as séances, Ouija boards, psychic powers, channeling, Wicca, "out-of-body" experiences, demonology, witchcraft, and astral projection.

Modern Americans want assurance

I remember when *Embraced By the Light* spent many weeks on the *New York Times* best-seller list in 1993 and 1994. Why did Americans gobble it up? Because most people want assurance of life beyond the grave. Saturated with New Age notions, it is the author's account of her "out of body experience," or as some others call it, "near death experience."

Why are these many tools of Spiritism so appealing, so alluring? They appeal to the sophisticated as well as the less educated. Voodoo and its assorted witchcraft might captivate the uneducated, but channeling, out-of-body experiences, astral projection, even the Ouija board, fascinate the most educated.

At the Naval Medical Center in Portsmouth, VA, a registered nurse is also the "pagan resource" person—the man who is called upon "to offer spiritual aid to patients who describe themselves as witches, Wiccans, Odinists, or followers of other Earth-centered belief systems. ... On behalf of pagan servicemen and servicewomen, Harris has handcrafted and consecrated healing talismans, cleansed hospital rooms of negative energy, and helped arrange healing rituals by covens."[18]

In a very instructive article in *Christianity Today*, Marvin Olasky, professor at the University of Texas (Austin), quotes historian Frank Podmore in listing four major reasons for Spiritism's appeal:

1) "The ranks of the Spiritualists were naturally recruited, largely from those who had freed themselves entirely from the Christian

---

18. Associated Press, March 18, 2002.

tradition, and had therewith lost all definite hope or belief in a future life."

2) "Some flocked to spiritism because within it there was no real good or evil, and no sin. People could follow their 'naturally benevolent instincts.' "

3) "Spiritist showmanship was appealing."

4) "Spiritism certainly appealed to those who had lost a spouse or child and hoped beyond hope to converse with the dead."

Olasky ends his article by saying that "those who try to syncretize New Age and Christian doctrines, either by proclaiming humanity's essential goodness or recommending 'visualization' techniques that place us at the center of things, should not be allowed to be church leaders."[19] It seems to me that he would have made his case stronger if he, himself, did not believe in an "immortal soul"! In the end time, we can expect Satan's brilliance to dazzle the senses of all, the sophisticated and the less educated, in a way that has never yet been seen on this planet. "So closely will the counterfeit resemble the true that it will be impossible to distinguish between them except by the Holy Scriptures. By their testimony every statement and every miracle must be tested."[20] Why? Because impersonations of departed loved ones, astounding healings, and shocking miracles of all kinds will overwhelm everyone who is not grounded in biblical truth.

Well–known Leaders

Many are the faithful followers of Spiritualism who are also well-known political leaders—such as William Lyon Mackenzie King, Canada's longest serving Prime Minister. King was most pleased with what he considered to be communications with his mother, father, siblings, and famous contemporaries. In his June

---

19. *Christianity Today*, December 14, 1992. Between 1990 and 2001, Wiccans have jumped 1,572 percent, from 8,000 to 134,000 self-proclaimed witches.—*USA Today*, December 24, 2001.

20. *The Great Controversy*, 593

30, 1932, diary, he wrote, "There can be no doubt whatsoever that the persons I have been talking with were the loved ones and others I have known and who have passed away. It was the spirits of the departed."

Another prominent world leader was Lord Dowding, commander of Great Britain's R.A.F during the Battle of Britain. Through a medium friend, many of the dead airmen were able to give their former Chief convincing evidence of their "survival." Lord Dowding would then pass on compassionate messages to the families of their dead relatives.

Who decided the exact time when President Reagan and Premier Gorbachev would sign the intermediate range nuclear forces treaty? According to *Time's* cover story "Astrology in the White House," (December 7, 1987) the astonishing answer seems to be the astrologer Joan Quigley, a 60-year-old Vassar graduate who has written three books on astrology.

Donald Regan, the former White House Chief of Staff, has written:

"Virtually every major move or decision the Reagans made during my time as White House chief of staff was cleared in advance with a woman in San Francisco who drew up horoscopes to make certain that the planets were in a favorable alignment for the enterprise."[21]

First Lady Nancy Reagan dabbled in astrology as far back as 1967. Her trust in astrology, however, was bolstered in 1981 when Quigley showed her that the astrologer's chart predicted extreme danger for the President around March 30. On that date, John Hinckley had severely wounded the President with a handgun. From that time on, Mrs. Reagan consistently consulted her astrologer to determine "propitious" times for her husband to travel, to make public appearances, and even to sign treaties.[22]

A subheading of *Time* rightly commented, "A strange mix of

22. Donald T. Regan, *Time*, May 16, 1988.

23. Barrett Seaman, *Time*, May 24, 1988.

spirituality and superstition is sweeping across the country."[23] How right they were!

It's no longer "fraudulent"

In 1951, Great Britain passed the Fraudulent Mediums Act, repealing the 1735 Witchcraft Act. Spiritualists may now openly and legally practice their religion. Great Britain today has more than 500 Spiritualist churches.[24]

One of the many venues for Spiritualistic gatherings is the Burning Man Festival, an annual six days in Black Rock Desert, 120 miles north of Reno, Nevada, the week prior to and including Labor Day weekend. The themes in past years include Fertility, Time, Hell, Outer Space, The Body, The Floating World, Beyond Belief, the Vault of Heaven, and Psyche.

The theme for 2006 is Hope and Fear. Recent attendance at The Burning Man surpassed 15,000 wiccans, satanists, goddesses (white witches), nudists, and a consortium of other partygoers who converged on the hot Nevada desert for a weekend of "glorious Hell on earth." The number of participants at the Burning Man gala has nearly doubled each year since 1986, and this year organizers hope to break an attendance of 30,000. The Burning Man is a no-holds-barred New Age "Woodstock" style festival, where neo-pagans, wiccans, transvestite entertainers, and back-slidden Christians go to trance, perform rituals, burn sacrifices to pagan gods and goddesses, dance in the nude, engage in sex, and otherwise "express" themselves and become one with Gaia (Mother Earth).

Melding Element

In the end times, Spiritualism will be the melding element that unites Protestants and Catholics. Again, why? Because both groups, with few exceptions, have bought Satan's lie regarding the

---

23. Friedrich, op. cit.

24. Some affiliated with the Spiritualists National Church, others with Christian Spiritualist Union or the Greater World Christian Spiritualists Associations, plus many independent churches.

immortal soul. Because of this common bond, it will be easier for these two groups to join together on an international Sunday law.

But more than astounding miracles (which are only window dressing), the real point, the grand finale—Satan himself appears impersonating Christ. After all the other "wonders" sponsored by Spiritualism, why would anyone doubt this Grand Impersonation?

What is Ellen's last word of counsel to us today as we face the stupendous climax to Satan's first lies and deceptions on Planet Earth—the Big Lie that Eve fell for: "You will not surely die" (Genesis 3:4)?

"Only those who have been diligent students of the Scriptures and who have received the love of the truth will be shielded from the powerful delusion that takes the world captive. By the Bible testimony these will detect the deceiver in his disguise. To all the testing time will come. By the sifting of temptation the genuine Christian will be revealed. Are the people of God now so firmly established upon His word that they would not yield to the evidence of their senses? Would they, in such a crisis, cling to the Bible and the Bible only? Satan will, if possible, prevent them from obtaining a preparation to stand in that day. He will so arrange affairs as to hedge up their way, entangle them with earthly treasures, cause them to carry a heavy, wearisome burden, that their hearts may be overcharged with the cares of this life and the day of trial may come upon them as a thief."[25]

Our only defense will be Bible truth in the head, firmly in place through much study and sharing and personal commitment. We may have lived a lifetime believing only that which we have personally seen and experienced. But eyes and ears will not be a safe defense in the face of "undeniable evidence" that loved ones have reappeared, pleading with God's loyalists to forget their so-called biblical doctrines that now seem so divisive in a world seeking harmony and tolerance of everybody else's "religion".

The appeal of "departed" loved ones—*that we should really*

---

25. Ibid., 625.

believe what we "see and hear"—will be almost overwhelming, even to the most intelligent Bible student. It will be a time when one's future absolutely will hang on believing the Word of the Lord and the counsel of His last-day messenger, Ellen White.

♦ CHAPTER SIX ♦

The Logical Plea— Can't We All Get Along?

S ometimes we can look at a Bible text or hear it quoted for years until we might as well be reading the alphabet. One of those texts is Paul's warning regarding earth's last days: "That in the last days perilous times will come for men will be lovers of themselves ... having a form of godliness but denying its power. ... For the time will come when they will not endure sound doctrine, but according to their own desires, because they have itching ears, they will heap up for themselves teachers; and they will turn their ears away from the truth, and be turned aside to fables" (2 Timothy 3:1, 2, 5; 4:3, 4).

Paul is giving us a heads-up! The old veteran is not talking about what will be going on in Buddhism, Hinduism, or Mohammedanism. He is warning the Christian church that in the end-time the gospel that turned the world upside down in the first century (Acts 17:6) would become so watered down that the secret of its power would be muted.

In the last days, Christians will seek teachers and preachers who will focus on their "felt" needs, rather than their "real" needs. They will want our Lord's name but not His character. They would prefer to "feel" their religion rather than build reasons for their faith that was once delivered to the first-century loyalists (Jude 3).

Let's take a look at what has been happening in Evangelical Protestantism during the past 20 years. One of the most remarkable legacies is the emergence of new types of worship services and the burst of mega-churches throughout the United States. A tsunami wave of books such as *Purpose Driven Life* and *Your Best Life Now* are heralded around the world for their practical, spiritual counsel, heavily buttressed with biblical texts. So what's the problem?

Something deeper is going on. The shift in the last half of the 20th century is not from its historical defense of the Bible's accuracy to modern liberalism, as it was in the first half of the last century. The shift now is from its traditional biblical base to a more psychological, sociological base, heated by the philosophies of pragmatism and New Spirituality. Of course, the Bible is used, but it is often not only misquoted and mistranslated, it becomes a grab bag to support whatever concept the user chooses to promote.

That is the new twist. For more than a century, as liberal Protestants have jettisoned the Bible as a reliable spiritual authority, today's Evangelicals, once the guardians of the authority of Scripture, do not deny the Bible itself, but rather, by its use, give the appearance that the Bible is not really that important on certain points. That makes only a short step then to other sources of truth that seem more relevant, more personal, more satisfying.

History seems to show that when those looking for authentic spirituality do not find it in places where the authority of the Bible is upheld, they will seek elsewhere for some kind of authority for their personal assurance. And few return to their traditional church services because they feel burned over with dry and irrelevant sermons, boring liturgies, and repetitive traditions. Such seekers, and they are many in *all* churches, still look for something that seems more personally satisfying without changing the language and feel of Christianity—and that is exactly what is happening. Many pastors, realizing this spiritual desert, search for the next spiritual experience that will validate their ministries.

Newsweek (August 29, 2005) recently featured a cover story called "In Search of the Spiritual." The subtitle was: "Move over, politics. Americans are looking for personal, ecstatic experiences of God, and, according to our poll, they don't much care what the neighbors are doing."

The New Spirituality emphasis has captured the attention and commitment of a great number of younger people especially. New Spirituality promises contact with God in ways not experienced in other, more conventional Christian paths.

Distinguish Between Spiritualism and Spirituality

We must distinguish between age-old Spiritualism and rampant New Spirituality. As we noted in chapter five, Spiritualism is the open appeal to find Reality, God, Cosmic Consciousness, whatever, through the *direct* contact with the "other" world. It could be through channeling, ouija boards, séances, certain kinds of extra-sensory perception, etc.

New Spirituality, at this point in time, doesn't go in that direction although it has much in common with Spiritualism. Both concepts or movements, however, believe in either the immortal soul or the subjective ability to find God or reality within themselves through any number of modalities. Neither believes in the final authority of Scripture.

Modern Mood in the 21st Century

Pollster George Gallup stated in his book, *The New American Spirituality*, that spirituality is very much alive, but it is without biblical foundation: "Contemporary spirituality can resemble a grab bag of random experiences that does little more than promise to make our eyes mist up or our heart warm. We need perspective to separate the junk food from the wholesome, the faddish from the truly transforming."[1]

The problem, as Gallup sees it, is the massive level of biblical

---

1. (Colorado Springs: Victor, 2000) 15.

illiteracy among Christians generally throughout the world. "Half," he says, "of those describing themselves as Christians are unable to name who delivered the Sermon on the Mount. Many Americans cannot name the reason for celebrating Easter or what the Ten Commandments are. People think the name of Noah's wife was Joan, as in Joan of Ark."[2]

Then Gallup describes the "great disconnect"—the wide gulf between what Americans in general and Christians in particular *claim to believe* and how they *actually live.* So he concluded that this "cluster of moral and theological shortcomings seemingly throws into question the transforming power of religious beliefs," leading Gallup to state, "just because Americans claim they are more spiritual does not make them so."[3] And then he asks the burning question: "Is the church really rediscovering its spiritual moorings, or just engaging in retreat from seemingly insoluble problems?"[4]

Filling the Vacuum

Whether the typical church is doing its job or not is a no-brainer. Most people are spiritually hungry, and they will find some spiritual guru who promises to satisfy their innate spiritual search. Itching ears will find teachers to satisfy their desires (2 Timothy 4:3).

That is why the tsunami wave of New Spirituality is sweeping over the American church. It comes in many forms. For many, if not most of the mega-churches, as expressed in their web networks and books they endorse, are riding this wave though they might not know its pending disaster in the endtimes.

Promoters of New Spirituality generally are gracious, charming, and in a way, very believable. They believe what they say; they believe that what they have experienced should be shared with the world. And much of what they say is indeed appealing. And the

---

2. Ibid., 30.

3. Ibid., 32, 29.

4. Ibid.

sale of their books proves it! The issue here, however, is that New Spirituality's focus and emphasis are light years away from biblical teaching.

John MacArthur, well-known pastor and author in southern California, summed up this tsunami drift: "The evangelical consensus has shifted decidedly in the past two decades. Our collective message is now short on doctrine and long on experience. Thinking is deemed less important than feeling. ... The love of sound doctrine that has always been a distinguishing characteristic of evangelicalism has all but disappeared. And a dose of mysticism to this mix and you have the recipe for unmitigated spiritual disaster."[5]

The Age of Aquarius

As we have discovered in the past 40 years, the term "New Age" is synonymous with "The Age of Aquarius." The central teaching of each phrase is that we are supposed to understand, one way or another, that God is within each person and can be found. The New Age movement that seemed so radical in the '60s and '70s did not die out. Rather, it integrated into society seemingly everywhere—medicine, business, schools, science, and finally even the last frontier, the evangelical church. Though the banner is no longer "New Age," its key elements have morphed in even greater degree into this pervasive New Spirituality.[6]

This book is not an attempt to explain fully New Age thought but to alert you of how and through whom New Age concepts are creeping into the pulpits and seminaries of *all* churches everywhere. Usually new movements or changes within Christianity come with great leaders proclaiming new ways to look at the "gospel," such as Reformation leaders and later John Wesley. But the New Age sneaks in like cancer. Beginning unnoticed, it gradually eats away and finally takes over the whole body unless it is recognized for

---

5. *Reckless Faith* (Wheaton, IL: Crossway Books, 1994), 154, 155.

6. One of the most lucid books on how New Spirituality is changing the face of Christianity is Ray Yungen's *A Time of Departing* (Silverton, OR: Lighthouse Trails Publishing Company, 2002).

what it is. Cancer treatment is not pleasant but necessary. Or the body eventually dies.

For many evangelical churches, New Age concepts were first rejected, then welcomed in parts, but eventually most of the former evangelical churches have become the "New Age Church" without many voices recognizing the cancer. Ears have been tickled. Most do not realize that they are full of cancer but live on in bliss with their New Age anesthetic.

New Spirituality Feeders

M. Scott Peck

Author of one of the best sellers of all time, *The Road Less Traveled*, Scott Peck's various books occupy a substantial share of bookstore space under "Self-help." When the book was first published, I was an instant admirer. (In fact, his *People of the Lie*[7] is still the best book I have ever read in analyzing evil.)

But when I reached his question, "What does God want from us?" and then his answer, "It is for the individual to become totally, wholly God,"[8] I knew something troubling was happening, although at that time, I was unclear about his New Age journey.

Among many other citations, Peck wrote in his book, *A World Waiting to Be Born*: "This process of emptying the mind is of such importance it will continue to be a significant theme. ... It may help to remember, therefore, that the purpose of emptying the mind is not ultimately to have nothing there; rather it is to make room in the mind for something new, something unexpected, to come in. What is the something new? It is the voice of God."[9] Further, Jesus was "an example of the Western mystic [who] integrated himself with God," that Jesus' message to us was "cease clinging to our lesser selves [and find]

---

7. (New York: Simon & Schuster, 1985) 1-269.

8. (New York: Simon & Schuster, 1978), 283.

9. (New York: Bantam Books, 1997), 88-89.

our greater true selves." Contemplative prayer[10] "is a lifestyle dedicated to maximum awareness."[11]

Michael D'Antonio, secular journalist, in his book *Heaven on Earth*, wrote that he saw Peck as "becoming the Billy Graham of the New Age ... a major New Age leader."[12]

Thomas Merton

Thomas Merton (1915–1968) has probably influenced New Age Spirituality more than any other person in the 20th century. And he's probably the most quoted by promoters of the New Spirituality. Roman Catholics highly praise Merton's works. One classic reference sets forth Merton's core belief: "It is a glorious destiny to be a member of the human race ... now I realize what we all are. ... If only they [people] could all see themselves as they really are. ... I suppose the big problem would be that we would fall down and worship each other. ... At the center of our being is a point of nothingness which is untouched by sin and by illusions, a point of pure truth. ... It is in everybody. This little point ... is the pure glory of God in us."[13]

Henri Nouwen

A Dutch Catholic priest (1932–1996), Henri Nouwen authored 40 books on the spiritual life. A *Christian Century* magazine survey conducted in 2003 indicated that Nouwen's work was a first choice for Catholic and mainline Protestant clergy.

Nouwen is praised for his warm, comforting appeal and impressive piety. But he walked firmly on the path of New Spirituality. Note his

---

10. Contemplative prayer is not biblical prayer, no matter how spiritual it sounds. Rather, It is a turning off our minds—putting them into neutral, in order to experience "the silence." Throwing our minds out of gear, trusting God to fill it, not only has no biblical warrant, but is an open door to spiritual deception. Paul said, "I shall pray with the spirit, and I shall pray with the mind" (1 Corinthians 14:15).

11. Ibid., 83.

12. New York: Crown Publishing, 1992), 342, 352.

13. *Reflections of a Guilty Bystander* (Garden City, New York: Doubleday, 1966), 140ff.

endorsement of the mantra[14], a common thread in New Spirituality: "The quiet repetition of a single word can help us to descend with the mind into the heart. ... This way of simple prayer ... opens us to God's active presence."[15]

Or in *Bread for the Journey*: "Prayer is 'soul work' because our souls are those sacred centers where all is one. ... It is in the heart of God that we can come to the full realization of the unity of all that is."[16]

Nouwen and Merton believed that their priestly experiences with silence was something that Protestants should understand—they should get the blessing of silence, shorthand for contemplative prayer.

Thomas Keating and Basic Pennington

Keating and Pennington, two Catholic monks, have written a number of popular books on contemplative prayer, such as *Centered Living, The Way of Centering Prayer*, and *Open Mind, Open Heart*. In *Finding Grace at the Center*, they wrote: "We should not hesitate to take the fruit of the age-old wisdom of the East and 'capture' it for Christ. Indeed, those of us who are in ministry should make the necessary effort to acquaint ourselves with as many of these Eastern techniques as possible. ... Many Christians who take their prayer life seriously have been greatly helped by Yoga, Zern, TM, and similar practices, especially where they have been initiated by reliable teachers and have a solidly developed Christian faith to find inner force and meaning to the resulting experiences."[17] Pennington wrote, "The soul of the human family is the Holy Spirit."[18]

---

14. Mantra, as used in Eastern religions and New Age thought, means a repeated word or phrase. The basic process is to focus and maintain concentration without thinking about what one is thinking about. Conscious thinking is gradually tuned out until an altered state of consciousness is achieved.

15. *The Way of the Heart* (San Francisco: Harper, 1981), 81,

16. (San Francisco: Harper, 1997), January 15, November 16.

17. (Petersham, MA: St. Bede's Publishing, 1978) 5, 6.

18. *Centered Living, The Way of Centering Prayer* (New York: Doubleday, 1986), p. 104.

Gerald May

Gerald May, psychiatrist, is known for his leadership in the Christian 12-step field and for being a cofounder and teacher in the Shalem Prayer Institute in Washington, D.C. The Institute is a powerful leader in contemplative prayer. Admittedly strongly influenced by Eastern religions, he wrote in *Addiction and Grace* (acclaimed as a classic in addiction recovery) that "our core ... one's center ... is where we realize our essential unity with one another and with all God's creation." He then states how this is achieved: "I am not speaking here of meditation that involves guided imagery or scriptural reflections, but of a more contemplative practice in which one just sits still and stays awake with God."[19]

In his *The Awakened Heart* he made it even clearer that he is clearly in the mystical panentheistic[20] camp when he talks about "cosmic presence" as revealed in "the Hindu greeetings of jai bhagwan and namaste that reverence the divinity that both resides within and embraces us all."[21]

John Main

John Main, a Benedictine monk (1926–1982), seems to be quoted by most everyone in New Spirituality. He popularized contemplative prayer as the "way of the mantra" first taught to him by a Hindu monk.[22] In 1977, he and Laurence Freeman founded a monastery in Montreal dedicated to a revival of ancient prayer modalities, chief of which is repeating a mantra. Ma-ra-na-tha, an Aramaic word that means "Come, Lord Jesus," is often chosen for their mantras. Today, Ottawa has become the Canadian capital for Chrsitian meditation

---

19. (San Francisco: Harper, 1988), 102, 166.

20. Panentheism combines the classic theism (a personal God) with pantheism (God is impersonal, pervading all creation). Panentheism is the foundational worldview of those engaged in mystical, contemplative prayer—God's presence in all things. That is why so many New Spirituality leaders talk about "all is one."

21. (San Francisco: Harper, 1991) 179.

22. "Lives of the Heart and Soul," *Maclean's* magazine, September 17, 1987, 42.

with practitioners in at least 114 countries. Australia alone has 300 groups throughout the country.

Matthew Fox

Matthew Fox, once a Catholic priest, now Episcopalian, has written more than two dozen books and developed an enormous following in Catholic and Protestant circles. He is a much-sought speaker, especially in New Age circles, emphasizing his panentheistic views.

Evangelical Hybrids

Richard Foster

One of the most well known of the New Spirituality Movement, Richard Foster, the founder of Renovaré, is committed to working for the renewal of the Church of Jesus Christ in all her multifaceted expressions. Renovaré holds regional and local conferences bringing together Christians across denominational lines for renewal. Foster's best known books include *Celebration of Discipline* (hailed by *Christianity Today* as one of the 10 best books of the 20th century[23]), *Streams of Living Water, Freedom of Simplicity*, and *The Challenge of the Disciplined Life*.

Of course, Foster has much that is devotionally helpful. But it doesn't take long to realize that Foster advocates a prayer movement that indeed can be proven to have strong links to Eastern mysticism.[24] Contemplative prayer, saturated with New Age, Eastern mysticism, universalism, and pantheism, is now infiltrating Christianity big time. In addition to his own writings, Foster has a great proclivity to quote or endorse others who are closely linked to Buddhism, such as the Catholic mystic Thomas Merton, whom he quotes 13 times in *Celebration of Discipline*. Merton wrote, "I think I couldn't understand Christian

---

23. *Christianity Today*, April 24, 2000.

24. "Every distraction of the body, mind, and spirit must be put into a kind of suspended animation before this deep work of God upon the soul can occur." *Celebration of Discipline* (San Francisco: Harper, 1978 edition) 13.

teaching the way I do if it were not in the light of Buddhism."[25]

In the back of *Celebration of Discipline,* Foster listed Tilden Edward's book *Spiritual Friend* as an "excellent book on spirituality." Edward's position is well known: "This mystical stream [contemplative prayer] is the Western bridge to Far Eastern spirituality."[26]

I mention Thomas Merton and Tilden Edward only as an example of many other indisputable Christian mystics, such as Dallas Willard, Calvin Miller, Madame Guyon, and John of the Cross, that Foster interchanges with—those also who are heavily indebted to Eastern mysticism, especially Buddhism. The fascinating as well as alarming factor here is that Foster and others wrap their particular goals and methodologies with biblical words so that average readers feel they are truly being blessed. In fact, many Evangelicals would be disturbed by the charge that Foster is promoting a pseudo-Christian mysticism.[27]

Most people only read the froth of Foster and don't think twice about what he says regarding visualization, one of the modalities of finding "reality" within: "You can actually encounter the living Christ in the event. It can be more than an exercise of the imagination, it can be a genuine confrontation. ... Jesus Christ will actually come to you."[28]

Further, "In your imagination allow your spiritual body, shining with light, to rise out of your physical body ... up through the clouds into the stratosphere ... deeper and deeper into outer space until there is nothing except the warm presence of the eternal Creator."

---

25. Frank X. Tuon, *The Dawn of the Mystical Age* (New York: Crossroad Publishing Co., 1997), p. 127.

26. *Spiritual Friend,* (New York: Paulist Pres, 1980), 18.

27. In *Christianity Today,* October 2005, Richard J. Foster and Dallas Willard were interviewed in "The Making of the Christian." If one read only this article, he or she would have no idea what kind of philosophies and methodologies for which these two gracious men are known. It shows again that most anybody can be received with open arms if they continue to use conventional Christian terms in promoting their core messages that do not begin with the authority of the Bible.

28. *Celebration of Discipline* (San Francisco: Harper, 1988), 26.

Then he goes on to say that this is more than imagination, but reality created with the mind.[29]

Brennan Manning

Brennan Manning is a delightful ex-Catholic priest who wrote *The Ragamuffin Gospel*, an emotionally gripping focus on God's forgiving nature and His love for the unworthy—but he works with a limited gospel. He like Foster has struck a responsive chord among Evangelicals who buy into his pleasing, passionate graciousness.

In his *Signature of Jesus*, Manning characterizes a contemplative spiritualist as one who "looks upon human nature as fallen but *redeemed*, flawed but in essence good."[30] He wrote, "The first step in faith is to stop thinking about God at the time of prayer."[31] The second step is "without moving your lips, repeat the sacred word [or phrase] inwardly, slowly, and often." If distractions come, "simply return to listening to your sacred word."[32] He also encourages his readers to "celebrate the darkness" because "the ego has to break; and this breaking is like entering into a great darkness."[33]

Manning strongly supports Basil Pennington's book on *Centering Prayer*, saying that Pennington's methods provide "a way of praying that leads to a deep living relationship with God."[34]

Other Best-selling New Spirituality Authors

Leonard Sweet's[35] *Soul Tsunami* is filled with positive quotes and material from New Agers and globalists such as James Redfield, author of *The Celestine Prophecy*, Sarah Ban Breathnach, Annie Dillard, Tome Sine, Wayne Dyer, and countless other well-known mystics and/or New Agers.

---

29. Ibid., 27.

30. *Signature of Jesus* (Colorado Springs, CO: NavPress, 2002), 125.

31. Ibid., 212.

32. Ibid., 218.

33. Ibid., 145.

34. Back cover, *The Ragamuffin Gospel* (Sisters, OR: Multnomah Press, 1990).

This passage from Sweet's *Quantum Spirituality* is common to New Spirituality: "If I find Christ, I will find my true self and if I find my true self, I will find Christ."[36] Sincere Christians should pause and ask three questions:

1) Should Christians run from basic biblical principles (in their rejection of dry sermons and stale church programs) to cutting-edge, exotic New Spirituality just because it couches its language in Christian terms, promising a fresh devotional life?

2) Should Christians allow the "instant gratification" appeal that permeates modern living embrace our spiritual connection with the God of the Bible—a very personal Father, Son, and Holy Spirit? Lasting friendships with other people take time to nurture, to learn all one can about the other. New Spirituality promises a new kind of "instant" gratification in the mantras of contemplative prayers.

3) Should Christians fall for what "works"—a phenomenal shift of the last century, not only in politics or science, but also in the religious world?

The Christian world once believed, generally, that truth is determined about what God has said and not on what seems to work "for me." The test of truth should not be, "will it make me feel good about myself?" New Spirituality promises a self-actualized, self-fulfillment, and a union with God that is nowhere recommended in the Bible.

Bible "Endorsement"

Psalm 46:10 is frequently used to promote "listening" or contemplative prayers: "Be still and know that I am God." The DVD

---

35. Endorsement on the cover of Sweet's book *Soul Tsunami* (Grand Rapids: Zondervan, 1999). "Soul Tsunami shows us why these are the greatest days for evangelism since the first century." Sweet is well known for his focus on unity—a worldwide oneness reflected in the growing union between the East and the West. In Sweet's *Quantum Spirituality*, we read: "Energy-fire experiences take us into ourselves only that we might reach outside of ourselves. Metanoia is a de-centering experience of connected-ness and community." "The power of small groups is in their ability to develop the discipline to get people 'in-phase' with the Christ consciousness and connected with one another."—page 147.

36. Ibid., 125.

entitled *Be Still* bears the inscription of Psalm 46:10 on its case.[37]

But as one would for any text, read the whole Psalm. David is surely not emptying his mind from thought or words of any kind. Notice how the Psalm begins: "God is our refuge and strength, A very present help in trouble." Or verse eight: "Come, behold the works of the Lord." Ignoring context is dangerous.

Christian Colleges and Seminaries Promoting Contemplative and Emerging Spirituality

For those of us who have known these college and seminaries a few decades ago, all this is mind-boggling. This list includes: Assemblies of God Theological Seminary, Biola University, Canadian Mennonite University, George Fox University Seminary, Mars Hill Graduate School, Simpson University, Trinity Western University, Wheaton College Graduate School. For example, Assemblies of God Theological Seminary program is led by Earl Creps, whose syllabi include materials from Henri Nouwen, Brian McLaren, Ken Blanchard, Dan Kimball, Sally Morgenthaler, and Leonard Sweet.

An intriguing book

One of the most intriguing books published only days after September 11, 2001, is *From the Ashes—A Spiritual Response to the Attack on America*.[38] In the introduction, Steven Waldman wrote: "At times like this, we can all benefit from hearing a wide variety of voices. That is why we at Beliefnet, the leading multifaith Web site on religion and spirituality, teamed up with Rodale, Inc. to collect the most eloquent and wise voices across the faith spectrum."[39]

---

37. April, 2006, Fox Home Entertainment released the Be Still DVD, featuring Richard Foster, Dallas Willard, Calvin Miller, and Beth Miller—all with one main message: You cannot know God if you do not practice the art of going into the silence. That silence is not normal prayer, talking to a personal God, but a special state of mind induced through contemplative prayer that helps "believers" to avoid the addiction to use words. It seems that Beth Miller, a well-known Evangelical, was misled in not recognizing the intent of the other speakers on the CD and she issued a statement that said she does not promote mystical type/Eastern meditation.

38. Emmaus, Pa: Rodale Press, 2001.

39. Ibid., ix.

One of those "eloquent and wise voices" is Neale Donald Walsch, who wrote: "The Bible, which is only one of humanity's many sources of spiritual teaching, carries this message throughout, in both the Old Testament and the New. (Have we not all one father? Has not one God created us? Why then are we faithless to one another, profaning the covenant of our fathers?—Malachi 2:10 ... so we, though many, are one body in Christ, and individually members one of another,—Romans 12:5 ... Because there is one bread, we who are many are one body —1Corinthians 10:17).

"This is a message the human race has largely ignored. ...

"We must change ourselves. We must change the beliefs upon which our behaviors are based. We must create a different reality, build a new society. And we must do so not with political truths or with economic trusts, and not with cultural truths or even the remembered truths of our ancestors—for the sins of the fathers are being visited upon the sons. We must do with new spiritual truths. We must preach a new gospel, its healing message summarized in two sentences:

"We are all one.

"Ours is not a better way, ours is merely another way.

"This 15-word message, delivered from every lectern and pulpit, from every rostrum and platform, could change everything overnight."[40]

One of the Alliance's co-founders and member of its board of directors, Marianne Williamson, presented these New Age ideas on *The Oprah Winfred* shortly after September 11. She outlined a peace plan based on New Age principles that would be an "alternative to Armageddon." And she announced Walsch would soon be presenting his 5-Step Peace Plan.

Explosion of Peace Plans

What shall we make of all this and much more? Since September 11, 2001, this planet has seen an enormous explosion of peace

---

40. Ibid., 19-21.

plans based on a new gospel that is the only way to a true and lasting peace. And these plans are not mere wishes.

Let's be unequivocally clear: All of us seek peace. All of us want poverty, ignorance, and disease to be banished from this planet. Our challenge comes down to one question: What is the gospel message that permeates these various humanitarian-uplift plans?

Modern peace plans are magnificently organized and enchantingly deceptive. What better way could be devised to set up the world with a unified voice that would heap ridicule on any group that would try to expose their errors? Never before has the whole world been wired and connected as today—web-based computer systems, global cell-phone networks, greater international air travel, GPS systems, etc. A united voice, "one mind," would speak and immediately the whole world would see and hear![41]

Labyrinth

Another remarkable signal of New Spirituality is the "labyrinth"[42] that is being featured at many Evangelical conferences, especially where younger members are being attracted. Often called "A-maze-ing Prayer, the labyrinth feature seems to fill the hunger of those who turn from well-choreographed worship services, every

---

41. See chapter 3.

42. The labyrinth is a path usually designed with intricate passageways and blind alleys. The most famous labyrinth of ancient times was the Cretan lair of the mythological Minotaur. Turf labyrinths still exist in England, Germany, and Scandinavia and were linked to fertility rituals. The Roman Catholic Church adopted the practice, and Christians made their pilgrimages to cathedrals in Chartres, Rheims, or Amiens where they completed their spiritual journeys in the cathedral labyrinths. The patterns of the labyrinth are similar to Buddhist mandalas and Japanese Zen practice of kinhim "walking meditation." Jean Houston, in the early 1990s, introduced the Christian world again to the practice of seeking enlightenment though walking the labyrinth when she linked up with Lauren Artress, spiritual leader of Grace Cathedral in San Francisco—to bring people back to their center and allow them to experience "Spirit" for themselves. See www.gracecathedral.org/labyrinth/ Jean Houston is listed on the Internet as one of the top-10 New Age speakers in North America. Many participants at Gorbachev's State of the World forum in 1997 also walked the labyrinth at Grace Cathedral

minute filled with music, videos, and preaching. Walking the "labyrinth" offers a private, unhurried, mystery-filled, meditative experience.

It seems that hungry experience-seekers are like moths drawn to the flame, ever seeking to know "god" through some kind of spiritual experience. Something seems to click in this pursuit. If you were handed an Ouija Board and told that it has been totally redeemed by your spiritual leader and that it would bring you into a greater experience of God, would you take the occult device looking for the promised higher spiritual experience? The labyrinth is the same as the Ouija Board.

In Deuteronomy 12:1–4 and in Exodus 34:10–17, we are admonished not to use anything connected to pagan ritual. No question about it—such pagan gateways do lead to "spiritual" experiences of one's self and "god"—but it is the portal to the demonic if not carefully considered.

At the National Pastors Conference in San Diego, March 9–13, 2004, the labyrinth path was formed by black lines on a 35-foot square piece of canvas laid on the floor. Participants were given a CD player with headphones to guide the journey through the 11 stations on the passageway. They were told not to rush but to slow down, breathe deeply, and fully focus on God.

Later in 2004, Graceland at Santa Cruz, California, featured the labyrinth as part of its annual art event and sold "The Prayer Path" kit that transformed a room into a medieval prayer sanctuary. Leaders who promote these labyrinths rejoice that meditative prayer "resonates with hearts of emerging generations."

When I noticed that Zondervan Publishing Company, a leading New Spirituality publisher, sponsored the National Pastor's Convention in February 22–25, 2006, I wondered who else is publishing New Spirituality materials. To my surprise, I discovered so does Intervarsity Press, NavPress (Navigators), Multnomah Books, Integrity, Thomas Nelson, Bethany House, Harold Shaw, and Harper SF. If I listed all the books now available, most readers would be equally shocked—they are the up-front, best sellers wherever Christian books are sold!

What is most interesting is the common thread of breath prayers by labyrinth participants reflected in the best sellers. But let's summarize: What are the chief distinguishing characteristics of New Spirituality? Obviously, not every promoter of New Spirituality emphasizes each of these characteristics—but it is very easy to identify its promoters. We probably have said enough about the following marks of New Spirituality—each characteristic is worth an entire book.

▶ Functional denial of the authority of Scripture

▶ Feelings eclipse reason in seeking truth

▶ Contemplative, repetitive prayers

▶ Visualizations to discover inner power and guidance

▶ Abundant references to Roman Catholic mystics

▶ Ancient "disciplines" are to be recovered and celebrated

▶ Unmediated link to the absolute—"god" is within every one

▶ All paths lead to God

▶ Finding one's core—one finds the great mystery called "god."

"Insider" terms used by contemplatives

Like most experts in any field, "contemplatives" also enjoy some special knowledge that others don't have; they use "inside" language, which is clear to the initiated but means little to "outsiders." For instance, you can track this "inside" language by noting the following:

Spiritual formation, Spiritual disciplines, Beyond Words, Being in the Present Moment, Slow Prayer, Awareness of Being, Mantra, Inner Light, Divine Center, Practicing the Presence, Dark night of the soul, Centering Prayer, Centering, Ignation Contemplation, Spiritual Direction, Divine Mystery, A Thin Place, Ancient Prayer Practices, Yoga, Palms Up-Palms Down, Lectio Divina, The Jesus Prayer, Jesus Candles, Breath Prayers, Prayer Stations, Enneagrams,[43] Labyrinths

---

43. The Enneagram (or Enneagon) is a nine-pointed diametric figure which is used in a number of teaching systems. The figure is believed to indicate the dynamic ways that certain aspects of things and processes are connected and change.

Emergent Church Movement

Another feature of New Spiritualism, but using a different tack, is the "Emergent Church" movement that has caught fire within the last 10 years. It is a reaction against various forms of evangelicalism with its church-structured programs. They find common ground among those who are doing their spiritual searching in local bars, cafés, and other leisure centers. In other words, they are repotting Christianity on to new cultural and intellectual ground.

Some groups seem to emphasize being simple followers of Jesus, avoiding the congregational milieu. They tend to be suspicious of church hierarchy, doctrinal formulations; they talk of "emerging authority." They are less concerned about safeguarding boundaries; they use words such as "liquid" churches. And they are much more open to a wider sphere of activity than just evangelism.

One of the key "inside" terms is "cross over to the other side," or variations of these words. Brian McLaren emphasizes this concept in his book *The Church on the Other Side.*[44] Many followers use these terms to depict a radical break with historical evangelical thought and practice. McLaren goes beyond promoting a change in pastoral methods to deal with the "postmodern world." He challenges ministers to rethink their message, not just their methods.[45]

Postmoderns now insist that truth is no longer found in the objective teachings of the Bible but whatever the individual or community believes it is—truth is whatever is arrived at through consensus. In other words, contradiction with historical Christianity is not only acceptable, it is welcomed. However one says it, "crossing over to the

---

44. (Grand Rapids, MI: Zondervan, 2001).

45. Os Guinness said it well: "What happens ... is drastic. Truths or customs that do not fit in with the modern assumption are put up in the creedal attic to collect dust. They are of no more use. The modification or removal of offending assumptions is permanent. What begins as question of tactics escalates to a question of truth; apparently, the modern assumptions are authoritative. Is the traditional idea unfashionable, superfluous, or just plain wrong? No matter. It doesn't fit in, so it has to go." Prophetic Untimeliness: A Challenge to the Idol or Relevance (Grand Rapids, MI: Baker Book House, 2003), 58.

other side" means an upfront denial of the New Testament gospel. It makes one wonder what Jude would say today: "I found it necessary to write to you exhorting you to contend earnestly for the faith which was once for all delivered to the saints" (Verse 3).

Emergent Church leaders and Jewish leaders

Emergent Christian and Jewish leaders met in a first-ever meeting on January 16–17, 2006, at the Brandeis-Bardin Institute in Simi Valley, California, to think together in developing congregations that pushed beyond the traditional categories of "left" and "right." Prominent Emergent Christian theologian Brian McLaren (Author of *A New Kind of Christian*) met with Synagogue 3000's (S3K) leadership three times in recent months to discuss shared concerns, particularly surrounding attempts by younger Christians and Jews to express their spiritual commitments through social justice. "We have so much common ground on so many levels," he notes. "We face similar problems in the present, we have common hopes for the future, and we draw from shared resources in our heritage. I'm thrilled with the possibility of developing friendship and collaboration in ways that help God's dreams come true for our synagogues, churches, and world."

S3K stresses the importance of building committed religious identity across faith lines. "We inhabit an epic moment," he said, "nothing short of a genuine spiritual awakening. It offers us an opportunity unique to all of human history: a chance for Jews and Christians to do God's work together, not just locally, but nationally, community by community, in shared witness to our two respective faiths."

According to Emergent-U.S. National Coordinator Tony Jones, this meeting has historic possibilities. "As emerging Christian leaders have been pushing through the polarities of left and right in an effort to find a new, third way, we've been desperate to find partners for that quest," he said. "It's with great joy and promise that we partner with the leaders of S3K to talk about the future and God's Kingdom."[46]

The Emergent Church movement is not a fad; it will find

46. www.typepad.com/t/trackback/3822640

common ground across all denominational lines, especially among the young who search for new ways to express themselves in spiritual pursuits.

Marks of Emergent Church Movement

▶ Bible no longer ultimate authority for many well-known leaders

▶ Bible dumbed-down with emphasis on images and sensual experiences

▶ More emphasis on "what's in it for me" in the "here and now"

▶ More emphasis on kingdom of God on earth rather than on Christ returning

▶ Many bridges established that lead to unity with the Roman Catholic Church

▶ Christianity needs to be re-invented to provide "meaning" for this generation

▶ Trend toward ecumenical unity for world peace, many ways to God

Counterfeiting the Everlasting Gospel

What does New Spirituality have to do with "counterfeits" in the end time? A thoughtful writer wrote:

"Satan can present a counterfeit so closely resembling the truth that it deceives those who are willing to be deceived, who desire to shun the self-denial and sacrifice demanded by the truth; but it is impossible for him to hold under his power one soul who honestly desires, at whatever cost, to know the truth."[47]

Ellen White nailed this counterfeit gospel as she observed it developing in her day with its new cloak:

"There is a spurious experience prevailing everywhere. Many are continually saying, 'All that we have to do is to believe in Christ.'

---

47. *The Great Controversy*, 528.

They claim that faith is all we need. In its fullest sense, this is true; but they do not take it in the fullest sense. To believe in Jesus is to take him as our redeemer and our pattern. If we abide in him and he abides in us, we are partakers of his divine nature, and are doers of his word. The love of Jesus in the heart will lead to obedience to all his commandments. But the love that goes no farther than the lips is a delusion; it will not save any soul. Many reject the truths of the Bible, while they profess great love for Jesus; but the apostle John declares, 'He that saith, I know him, and keepeth not his commandments, is a liar, and the truth is not in him.' While Jesus has done all in the way of merit, we ourselves have something to do in the way of complying with the conditions. 'If ye love me,' said our Saviour, "keep my commandments.' "[48]

A counterfeit gospel will become a worldwide movement capturing the attention and praise of the media. It will be a limited gospel, a gospel of convenience that will satisfy modern "felt" needs. The consequence of a counterfeit limited gospel so prevalent today, especially in the seeker-friendly churches, is a church full of people enjoying the grace of forgiveness but with no clear grasp of the grace of power that will indeed make them into overcomers. One of the chief reasons for this limited understanding of the grace of power (Hebrews 4:16) is their cloudy understanding of why the commandments of God are essential to their salvation.

Larry Crabb, one of the best-known Christian counselors in America, is spiritual director for the 55,000-member American Association of Christian Counselors. His books are many. He predicted, "The spiritual climate is ripe. Jesus seekers across the world are being prepared to abandon the old way of the written code for the new way of the spirit." Tony Campolo, in his book *Speaking My Mind,* said that "mysticism (contemplative prayer) provides some hope for common ground between Christianity and Islam." A world united under the cloak of spiritualism and

48. *Historical Sketches of the Foreign Missions,* 188, 189; see *The Great Controversy,* 464.

New Spirituality is exactly what the biblical picture of the end times predicts.[49]

Summary

In the last 25 years, we have been watching a spiritual tsunami sweeping over North America. Called New Spirituality, much of the noted increase in spirituality across denominational lines as well as those who have bolted their former denominational ties is centered in finding meaning in life through personal, subjective feeling. General bookstores, as well as Christian markets, are

---

49. One example of many New Spirituality leaders is Alice Bailey. Note this excerpt from "The xternalization of the Hierarchy," Section II, The General World Picture: "The intelligent youth of all countries are rapidly repudiating orthodox theology, state ecclesiasticism and the control of the church. They are neither interested in man-made interpretations of truth nor in past quarrels between the major world religions. At the same time, they are profoundly interested in the spiritual values and are earnestly seeking verification of their deep seated unvoiced recognitions. They look to no bible or system of so-called inspired spiritual knowledge and revelation, but their eyes are on the undefined larger whole in which they seek to merge and lose themselves, such as the state, an ideology, or humanity itself. In this expression of the spirit of self-abnegation may be seen the appearance of the deepest truth of all religion and the justification of the Christian message. Christ, in His high place, cares not whether men accept the theological interpretations of scholars and churchmen, but He does care whether the keynote of His life of sacrifice and service is reproduced among men; it is immaterial to Him whether the emphasis laid upon the detail and the veracity of the Gospel story is recognized and accepted, for He is more interested that the search for truth and for subjective spiritual experience should persist; He knows that within each human heart is found that which responds instinctively to God, and that the hope of ultimate glory lies hid in the Christ-consciousness.

"Therefore, in the new world order, spirituality will supersede theology; living experience will take the place of theological acceptances. The spiritual realities will emerge with increasing clarity and the form aspect will recede into the background; dynamic, expressive truth will be the keynote of the new world religion. ... When the racial problem has disappeared through the recognition of the one Life, when the economic problem has been solved by the nations working cooperatively together, when the problem of right government within each nation has been determined by the free will of their respective peoples, and the spirit of true religion is unobstructed by ancient forms and interpretations, then we shall see a world in process of right experience, right human relations and a spiritual moving forward to reality." http://laluni.hellowyou.ws/netnews/bk/esternalisation/extel1087.html

awash with best-sellers that promote finding Reality within through contemplative prayer, walking labyrinths, and imaging the fulfillment of promises made by prosperity preachers.

Turned off by conventional churches that have lost their spiritual pulse, they also have turned off the Bible as a source of divine revelation. But these "turned-off" ones are not leaving the circle of Christianity to follow the occult world—they are helping the occult world remodel the Christian Church without realizing it. When clear Bible texts are made to say that "God is in everything and everything is in God," we should recognize the subtle deception that is flooding even Christian bookstores.

Never has a generation of young and old, of rich and poor, thrown themselves into the winds of subjectivism, hoping to satisfy their desires for spiritual warmth without self-denial. The world on all continents is being led to conform to a universal spirituality that proclaims the oneness of all, a brotherhood of "believers" who live in tolerance toward one another's religious beliefs because the Reality they worship is deeper than divisive doctrine. This global, unifying spirituality positions the world to welcome the Great Impersonator—Satan himself when he imitates the return of Jesus.

Last-day appeals of "Can't we all get along?" will be more than intimidating, they will be coercive, leading to the day when men and women who "don't go along" will not be able to "buy or sell." In fact, they will be condemned "to be killed" for their defense of truth (Revelation 13:15, 17).

"For the time will come when they will not endure sound doctrine, but according to their own desires, because they have itching ears, they will heap up for themselves teachers; and they will turn their ears away from the truth, and be turned aside to fables" (2 Timothy 4:3, 4).

"Many will come in My name, saying, 'I am the Christ,' and will deceive many" (Matthew 24:5).

For false christs and false prophets will rise and show great signs and miracles to deceive, if possible, even the elect. See, I have told you beforehand" (Matthew 24;24, 25).

Are we there yet?

Theme: Jesus will return when Satan has
reached maximum ferocity against
God's loyalists.

♦ CHAPTER SEVEN ♦

Evil, How Great Thou Art!

"**A**nd the dragon [the devil and Satan, vs. 9] was enraged with the woman [church], and he went to make war with the rest of her offspring, who keep the commandments of God and have the testimony of Jesus Christ" (Revelation 12:17).

"And then the lawless one will be revealed, whom the Lord will consume with the breath of His mouth and destroy with the brightness of His coming. The coming of the lawless one is according to the working of Satan, with all power, signs, and lying wonders, and with all unrighteous deception among those who perish, because they did not receive the love of the truth, that they might be saved" (2 Thessalonians 2:8–10).

In the Great Controversy between Christ and Satan, Satan caused the controversy, not God. Evil itself was not created—freedom was. Evil is the dark side of freedom; when anyone says no to God, it is a law that evil and its consequences are the sure result.

God's first-born, Lucifer (the "light bearer"), was created "full of wisdom and perfect in beauty"—"the seal of perfection" (Ezekiel 28:12, 13). Mentally, physically, emotionally, socially, spiritually—he had it all!

The first of all created intelligences, he was the "anointed cherub" (Ezekiel 28:14). He was "anointed" for a special purpose; he was God's Minister of Cosmic Communications—the "bearer of God's light of truth"—the angel closest to the Godhead. *Nothing* was hid from his gaze.

Think about it! Lucifer was immensely qualified to accurately represent the truth about God to all created intelligences that would eventually inhabit the universe. Did he not "walk[ed] up and down in the midst of the stones of fire" (Ezekiel 28:14)? Surely, he saw and felt it all!

He was that first link between the Creator and His creation. As God's light/truth bearer, his highest responsibility was to make God look good. Whenever a question would arise, Lucifer had the qualifications and the job description to represent God's position fully and correctly.

Could any created being ever have a more important, self-fulfilling responsibility?

The divine record says: "You were perfect in your ways ... till iniquity was found in you" (Ezekiel 28:15). How can anyone understand this proto–iniquity? Isaiah noted that Lucifer "said in his *heart*" (Isaiah 14: 13, emphasis added) that he desired a still higher position, still more power! Emotion prevailed over reason. Did he allow his pride and ambition to erode the divine bonding of trust and love?

Apparently, Lucifer grew weary of making God look good—he wanted some of that honor! He became less satisfied with his peerless privileges and wanted to be more than the executive vice president of the universe! However it happened, and as preposterous as it now seems, he began to lay plans to also "sit on the mount of congregation on the farthest sides of the north" and be recognized "like the Most High."

Power leads to control and the twilight of freedom

And so, for the first time in the universe of free intelligences, the craving for "power," the "desire for self-exaltation," emerged. How such feelings and thoughts could possibly arise in one so close to God is beyond human understanding. Paul called it "the mystery of iniquity" (2 Thessalonians 2:7). Though it is unfathomable, this fateful desire for self-exaltation and power sows seeds of coercion and control—somebody somewhere will lose freedom.

Whenever the passion for power emerges in history or in our own hearts, we hear Satan's words: "I will ascend ... I will exalt ... I will be like the Most High" (Isaiah 14:13, 14). The religion of power (it becomes the passion of all lives that are not committed to the power of God) is the antithesis of genuine Christianity. The desire for power not only permeates secular philosophies, it unfortunately pervades much of what we call Christian aspirations and service. To be considered "somebody," to have a name that sets one apart or above another, to be recognized as important (as symbolized with the corner office, or the designated parking place), becomes the primary, overriding passion in life, rising even above one's commitment to responsibility and integrity.[1]

Fueling Satan's lust for power were then mysterious feelings we now call jealousy, envy, and, inevitably, hatred. This prototype scenario is played out daily in those who have never been converted to Christ's way of looking at power and His example of how to use it.

Ezekiel wrote that Lucifer's iniquity, his vanishing rectitude, was also rooted in vanity—"Your heart was lifted up because of your beauty; You corrupted your wisdom for the sake of your splendor" (Ezekiel 28:17). Vanity is the other side of jealousy.

Slowly, imperceptibly, jealousy became envy and Lucifer began to rationalize (justify) his strange feelings. And his feelings became words—sly, devious, deceptive words. Lucifer, the brightest of all creation, was slowly, imperceptibly becoming Satan, the beginning of entropy[2] in a perfect universe.

---

1. See author's *God At Risk* (Roseville, CA: Amazing Facts, 2004), "Appendix C: The Heart of Power," 414-424.

2. "Entropy ... the steady degradation or disorganization of a system or society."—Webster's *Ninth Collegiate Dictionary*.

Jesus said that Lucifer became "the devil ... a murderer from the beginning ... no truth in him ... a liar, and the father of it" (John 8:44). John wrote that "he who sins is of the devil, for the devil has sinned from the beginning" (1 John 3:8). Hard to believe that Satan wanted to "be like the Most High" (Isaiah 14:14); actually he wanted to murder God and take His place as ruler of the universe. (How else could he take God's place?) He proved this by murdering Jesus!

John was told about this awful war that developed "in heaven" and how it affected Planet Earth: "Michael and his angels fought against the dragon; and the dragon and his angels fought, but they did not prevail, nor was a place found for them in heaven any longer. So the great dragon was cast out, that serpent of old, called the Devil and Satan, who deceives the whole world; he was cast to the earth, and his angels were cast out with him" (Revelation 12:7–9).

God created a perfect planet, everything was "very good" when the first human couple was created (Genesis 1:31). But we have lived through many thousands of years of what has happened since Satan was cast "to the earth."

Evil has bitter roots. Its consequences travel through the genetic stream. The history of this planet can be easily written as a chronicle of wars, bloodshed, suffering, and misery. Any way you figure it, "the wages of sin [evil] is death" (Romans 6:23).

But Planet Earth now is in its last days—never been this late before! We live in the days when the Great Controversy on this planet has reached its tipping point—Satan knows that he has a "short time" (Revelation 12:12). He is now enraged, furious with God's loyalists, pulling out all the stops on his organ of fury and hate (Revelation 12:13).

What are Satan's chief weapons? He has had many thousands of years of practice and experience, starting long before this earth was populated. We have his track record. He brought great grief to the heavenly family before he was "cast down" to this earth. He has been sharpening his skills ever since.

Satan's Four Integrated Skills

Satan is skilled in . . .

▶ the use of consistent, destructive lies (*pretense*);

▶ blaming others for the damage he is doing (*scapegoating*);

▶ clouding the issues; changing the meaning of words—the substitution of opinion for absolute truths (*confusion*);

▶ the use of power to control or destroy others (*coercion*).[3]

Anyone infected with self-centeredness (as Lucifer-turned-Satan was) soon develops intolerance to criticism, a bottomless hate for the reprover (whether God or man), an intellectual deviousness that glorifies the means rather than the end, and a ghastly use of power to coerce others. All the while, pretenders on the pathway of evil learn ways to act as if they are respectable, trustworthy, deeply concerned about the feelings of others, and, yes, the champions of individual rights and "freedom."

Scott Peck's *People of the Lie* is probably the most penetrating analysis of evil that I have ever read. For instance: "Evil was defined as the use of power to destroy the spiritual growth of others for the purpose of defending and preserving the integrity of our sick selves. In short, it is scapegoating."[4]

The end of all this evil (and all that Satan represents) is "to kill life." That is exactly the framework in which events in the last acts of the great controversy prior to our Lord's second advent will take place— "He was granted power to give breath to the image of the beast, that

---

3. These four integrated skills move in sequence, pretense to coercion. Pretenders always appear as up-front supporters, covering up their real motives. Otherwise, it would not be deceit or deceptive. When the issues become more public, the pretender continues his deception by blaming someone else for the "mess." When the "mess" involves more people and "sides" are being formed, the pretender continues his deceptions by confusing the issue, formulating new definitions for traditional words, always appearing to be supporting what he is destroying. When the pretender has enough followers, he uses deception again by appealing to the majority to silence the minority, one way or another.

4. M. Scott Peck, *The People of the Lie* (New York: Simon & Schuster, 1983), 119.

the image of the beast should both speak and cause as many as would not worship the image of the beast to be killed" (Revelation 13:15).

No Theological Theory

I am not speaking of theological theory. Nor of otherworldly, unseen deviltry. Satan's character has been incarnated many times throughout human history. Consider Josef Stalin. On November 7, 1937 (Revolutionary Day), after the military parade in Red Square, at the feast in Marshal Kliment Voroshilov's home, Stalin gave a toast that is remarkably honest and chilling—and everyone there knew exactly what he was saying for they all had lived through a ghastly bloodletting in which tens of thousands of Russian military leaders had been murdered:

"I would like to say a few words, perhaps not festive ones. The Russian tsars did a great deal that was bad. They robbed and enslaved the people. They waged wars and seized territories in the interests of landowners. But they did one thing that was good—they amassed an enormous state. ... We have united the state in such a way that if any part were isolated from the common-socialist state, it would not only inflict harm on the latter but would be unable to exist independently and would inevitably fall under foreign subjugation. Therefore, whoever attempts to destroy that unity of the socialist state ... is an enemy, a sworn enemy of the state and of the peoples of the USSR. And we will destroy each and every such enemy, even if he is an Old Bolshevik; we will destroy all his kin, his family. We will mercilessly destroy anyone who, by his deeds or his thoughts— yes, his thoughts—threatens the unity of this socialist state. To the complete destruction of all enemies, themselves and their kin!" Approving exclamations followed: "To the great Stalin!"[5]

Applying the Great Satan's Strategy to the Last Generation

How will Satan use *pretense*—the use of consistent, destructive lies—in attempting to destroy faith in the last days? After all, Jesus

---

5. The Diary of Georgi Dimitrov, the Bulgarian head of the Comintern, kept from 1933-1949. Cited in *The Wilson Quarterly*, Summer 2003, 114.

put His finger on one of the signs of the end times: "Nevertheless, when the Son of Man comes, will He really find faith on the earth" (Luke 18:8)?

What happens to individuals, legislatures, even Supreme Courts when arguments used are pretentious "lies" in respect to what they are supposed to be upholding? Why the pretense of honor, or love, or justice when someone's freedom is limited because of his or her color or religion?

In the family, we often see a spouse pretending love, all the while destroying the mate or child with suffocating control, searing blame, or outrageous, but believable, lies. In the military, we are told that we must "waste" a village to save a country. Even the U.S. Supreme Court had approved, in the name of a free America, imprisoning Jehovah Witnesses who chose not to salute the American flag (for religious reasons).[6] How many decades did the highest court in the United States classify American blacks as only two-thirds of a citizen and protected a slave-holder's ownership of slaves as personal property—in a country that told the world that "all men are created equal"?[7]

This is not the place to argue the past. We do, however, have a responsibility to discern the signs of the times, not only as citizens of the "land of the free and the home of the brave," but as students of prophecy. John the Revelator tells us that, in the end time, Satan and his followers, angels and humans, will exercise all their skill in making evil so deceptive that most of the world "marveled

---

6. 1940 Minersville School District v. Gobitis 310 US 586 (1940). The Court portrayed the case as balancing conflicting claims of liberty and authority. The school's interest in creating national unity was more important than the rights of the students to refuse to salute the flag. However, the Supreme Court overruled their previous decision in West Virginia Board of Education v. Barnette, 319 U.S. 624,1943, recognizing the fundamental right to religious liberty when it held that Jehovah's Witness schoolchildren could not be penalized when they refused to salute the American flag for religious reasons. In an opinion noted for its eloquence, Justice Robert H. Jackson wrote, "If there is one fixed star in our constitutional constellation, it is that no official, high or petty, can prescribe what shall be orthodox in politics, nationalism, religion, or other matters of opinion or force citizens to confess by word or act their faith therein."

7. Ibid. 384-391.

and followed the beast" as they beheld his amazing power and authority—and most of the world will join Satan, finally, in attempting to kill those who resist their lies.

Setting Up the United States

So how will Satan's lies set up the United States to be the world leader in uniting all nations under a religious authority that has universal clout and enough muscle to enforce economic hardship and persecution on those they hate? How will satanic lies become so believable that "the world worshiped the beast" (Revelation 13:4)?

▶ by pretense, consistent lies, though appearing to serve a noble purpose;

▶ by blaming those they hate for causing the national crises;

▶ by causing confusion in substituting policy for principle (the end justifies the means), substituting opinion for absolute truths, redefining the meaning of words;

▶ by employing various forms of coercion—and all to one end, the eradication of dissent and individual freedom.

In 2003, during the spring war in Iraq, we had a fascinating example of how masters of evil will always find an audience who will believe them, in spite of what seems to others as undeniable reality. The Iraqi Information Minister Mohamed Saeed al-Sahaf had been denying reports that U.S. Army and Marine forces were moving freely in the center of Baghdad, even when his listening audience could hear the coalition tanks nearby. He was assuring the Iraqi people that the Republican Guard was in control of the airport. Then he offered to take reporters to the airport to prove it! Of course, most of them had already been to the airport and had seen the coalition forces for themselves.

Day after day in early April 2003, the world awaited al-Safaf's latest daily virtuoso performance. Some of his comedic propaganda included: "They say they brought 65 tanks into the center of the city. I say to you it is not true. This is part of their sick mind. There is no presence of infidels in the city of Baghdad at all." (All the while he had to speak loudly because of the gunfire in the streets below his hotel.) Further, his daily ritual included, "U.S. troops were poisoned yesterday" and "U.S. troops are committing suicide."

Ted Simons commented, "We are entering an era in which the news media and the general public's adeptness at detecting and dissection spin in public discourse is matched only by the messengers' confusion. Put simply, it's hard, and getting harder, to know whom to believe."[8]

Blizzard Claims and Bias

This is just one analysis of what is behind and under the blizzard of false advertising claims, media bias, outrageous political accusations, and cheating scandals. In other words, it has become fashionable to deny truth, to scoff at any information that is contrary to personal opinion, to revise history, and to blame others for whatever happens. It clearly is a time when political correctness is legislating a new society of victims and tolerance for what once was unacceptable conduct.

In a time of moral confusion and financial crises, it would be a perfect time for certain leaders (who have made a career of beguiling others by appealing to their feelings, not their heads) to promise, in a fresh, captivating way, that they have the solution for peace, unity, and brotherhood of all mankind. This world has an uncanny ability to believe pretense!

Grandest Pretense of the Last Days

As we have been unfolding in this book, world conditions in the end time will be unprecedented. Natural disasters, economic impasse, and moral decadence will cause many to examine the causes of such unparalleled troubles. Just exactly how Satan has planned it:

> "Satan puts his interpretation upon events, and they think, as he would have them, that the calamities which fill the land are a result of Sundaybreaking. Thinking to appease the wrath of God

8. Editor-in-Chief, *Presentations* Magazine, March 2003.

[as they see it] these influential men make laws enforcing Sunday observance."[9]

This is a magnificent example of pretense. The same strategy that Satan used in capturing the confused mind of one-third of heaven's angels (Revelation 12: 4, 7,8) will work famously in confusing the world that *God's loyalists are the cause* of this world's terrible troubles. Pure pretense!

Scapegoating

The world's religious leaders, self-afflicted by their endorsement of Spiritualism (blindsided by the immortal-soul notion) and their ambivalence toward the Ten Commandments, will look for the "cause" and a solution for last-day crises, including "fast-spreading corruption." Their pretense (saluting the big lie) leads to Satan's use of his second strategic level—the look for a scapegoat. The age-old phenomenon of scapegoating shows up everywhere. It causes great anxiety and misery. Scapegoats are found in almost every social context: in school playgrounds, in families, in small groups, in churches, and in large organizations. Whole nations may be scapegoated. I like this technical definition:

> "Scapegoating is a hostile discrediting routine by which people move blame and responsibility away from themselves and towards a target person or group. It is also a practice by which angry feelings and feelings of hostility may be projected, via inappropriate accusation, towards others. The target feels wrongly persecuted and receives misplaced vilification, blame and criticism; he is likely to suffer rejection from those who the perpetrator seeks to influence. Scapegoating has a wide range of focus: from "approved" enemies of very large groups of people down to the scapegoating of individuals by other individuals. Distortion is always a feature."[10]

Ellen White summed up satanic strategy of scapegoating in the last generation:

> "Yet this very class [religious leaders] put forth the claim that the

---

9. *Last Day Events*, 129.

10. www.scapegoat.demon.co.uk

fast-spreading corruption is largely attributable to the desecration of the so-called 'Christian sabbath,' and that the enforcement of Sunday observance would greatly improve the morals of society. ... It is one of Satan's devices to combine with falsehood just enough truth to give it plausibility."[11]

What I am getting at is that a time of moral confusion and financial crises would be a perfect time for well-known leaders to promise, in fresh, captivating ways, that they have the solution for peace, unity, and brotherhood of all mankind (where everyone's opinion and lifestyle is equally as good as anyone else's). This cheap shot is common fare for most politicians—change the issue into finding a common culprit to blame. This ploy seems to dominate every newscast.

Hitler knew how to use the strategy of scapegoating in the early 1930s in Germany. Scapegoats are always available—just find those who may look different or worship differently. If the majority doesn't respond immediately to pretense and scapegoating, the tyranny of the minority will always gain power and lead the way. Hitler's Germany is a perfect paradigm of how events in the last of the last generation will develop!

In 1972, Rene Girard, a French literary critic, focused on the question of the *violent* root of culture through literature, anthropology, psychology, and biblical criticism. Through a succession of books and articles, he has pursued what he calls his *idée fixe:* the way in which *scapegoats* found, preserve, and unify culture. Girard found societies resort to acts of violence to restore order: "By organizing retributive violence into a united front against an enemy common to all the rivals, either an external enemy or a member of the community symbolically designated as an enemy, violence itself is transformed into a socially constructive force."[12]

Girard went on to say, "Where only shortly before, a thousand individual conflicts had raged unchecked between a thousand

---

11. *The Great Controversy,* 587.

12. James l. Fredericks, *The Cross and the Begging Bowl: Deconstructing the Cosmology of Violence." Buddhist-Christian Studies* 18 (1998), 155.

enemy brothers, there now reappears a true community, united in its hatred for one alone of its members. All the rancors scattered at random among the divergent individuals, all the differing antagonisms, now converge on an isolated and unique figure, the surrogate [scapegoat] victim."[13]

In the Great Controversy, scapegoating has been Satan's method over and over again—he rarely loses! Think of Caiaphus and Christ and Calvary. That same sinister mind will duplicate Calvary madness in the end time when "a true (?) community, united in its hatred for one alone of its members," declares that a member is expendable to save the larger community from pending chaos. For Jewish leaders, Jesus was expendable for the greater good!

Scapegoating becomes fully blossomed in the end time: "It will be declared that men are offending God by the violation of the Sunday sabbath; that this sin has brought calamities which will not cease until Sunday observance shall be strictly enforced; and that those who present the claims of the fourth commandment, thus destroying reverence for Sunday, are troublers of the people, preventing their restoration to divine favor and temporal prosperity."

Confusion

The confusion that Satan causes is seen everywhere where honesty, clarity, integrity, and truth are under fire. We see it when policy is substituted for principle (such as, the end justifies the means), or when opinion is substituted for absolute truths.

One of the most remarkable books of the 20th century, *1984*[14], by George Orwell (Eric Hugh Blair), described the totalitarian state where doublespeak reverses language and obliterates or revises history to suit the state—where freedom of thought is allowed to the masses because they don't think!

---

13. Rene Girard, *Violence and the Sacred* (Baltimore: The Johns Hopkins University Press, 1977), 79.

14. Published first in 1949 (hardback), later in paperback (Hammondsworth, England: Penguin Books, 1954, reprinted at least 26 times),

Three chapters are entitled "War is Peace", "Ignorance is Strength," and "Freedom is Slavery." Freedom is the "freedom to say two plus two equals five." The Ministry of Peace is actually the Ministry of War; joycamp is really the labor camp—examples that words mean the exact opposite of what they appear to mean. Orwell got some of his inspiration from Nazi Germany and Communist Russia, which had earlier employed some of the methods of *1984.* Yet much of the book has been thought of as an overview of time to come when the world generally will believe the Big Lie and falsify history—all leading to the attempted extinction of those guilty of thought crimes.

One of the classic confusions in language is "Sabbath" understood as Sunday. Both the late Pope John Paul II and his successor, Pope Benedict XVI, have written powerful epistles emphasizing the importance of the Christian's Sabbath worldwide—each time referring to Sunday.

Western nations are wrestling with the double meaning of "diversity" and "multiculturalism." Both are code words. Instead of a healthy respect for differences that made American a different kind of nation on earth, they are like "Trojan horses" that smuggle into general language the notion of moral relativism—code names for no such thing as right and wrong.

Remember the ridicule President Ronald Reagan received when he called the Russian empire "evil"? That was considered "judgmental!" When hate-filled, sex-saturated music and videos are the hottest items on the market, they are defended with language like "expression of youth culture." If one speaks up with Christian love, he or she is labeled "intolerant." It seems we embrace the lies and run from the truth, all for fear of offending someone.

"Religious freedom" becomes "freedom from religion" not "freedom of religion."

Gender is artificial discrimination, a mere invention of society—to argue differently exhibits intolerance. Transvestites exalt "selfhood," confusing the vulnerable young. Pro-choice for many means pro-murder. "Family Health" courses are taught in very early grades to teach "lifestyles" that are most often at odds with the "family health" of the young student's family.

"Hate speech" trumps "free speech," threatening any group on the basis of race, color, or religion. In other words, any book that criticizes another's religion in the interest of historical accuracy or biblical principles subjects the author and publisher to legal action. Such litigation already exists in numerous countries today.

"Progressive" once meant growth and openness but is now a code word used by the defense of a client's altercation with police supporting his client's ethnicity.[15] Or for church services that celebrated Evolution Sunday.[16] "Progressive theologians, for example, did not attack traditional views. They used traditional terminology and concepts but infused them with new meanings. ... But the arrival of R.H. Pierson to the General Conference presidency (1966) brought a dramatic change. The new administration concluded that the progressives threatened the very soul and mission of Adventism."[17]

In other words, liberals preferred to see themselves as "progressives," not conservatives, nor traditionalists. In other words, "progressive" has been morphed into what so many describe as avant-garde, the muting of authority, the relativity of values (such as "pride in progressive values," Hollywood style), and emphasizing innovation over tradition.

"Spirituality" becomes Novocain for young and old who want the soothing "presence" of God without accepting His moral code.

Bioethics that once stressed "sanctify of life" slips into an emphasis on "quality of life." Advocacy journalism has become a modern code word for opinion-directed news gathering, not objective reporting. "Minority" is condemned because it is insulting and implies inferiority. "Political correctness" is a code word for

---

15. CNN, March 31, 2006.

16. *Denver Post*, February 12, 2006.

17. *Spectrum*, Vol. 15, #2, pp 25, 26.

shutting down freedom of speech that aims for open and frank discussion. "Freedom of expression" becomes a cover for polluting the air with profanity and pornography. "Evangelical Christian," in some minds, becomes "Religious Right." "Freedom" becomes the right to be left alone. Or free to "do your own thing."

"Nofault" car insurance—where both the guilty and the innocent become victims and everybody gets to collect. Words such as "overweight" and "fat" are often put in quotation marks to isolate these terms as used by intolerant outsiders who want to impose their own standards. Even "stoutness" has become a no-no. A deaf person is "hearing disadvantaged."[18]

Universal victimhood becomes universal innocence. Increasing numbers of juries do not feel rage but pity; they look beyond proof of guilt and focus on the disadvantages in the life of the victimizer. It seems that one can do whatever—murder, rape, arson—as long as one says he or she is sorry!

Perhaps *1984* was far more prophetic than even Orwell's most devoted followers envisioned. Language now needs a new dictionary every 10 years!

Satan is "slick," with plenty of practice in causing confusion! Remember—he is an expert on turning minds from the truth, from listening to the voice of God in the soul, anything to keep people from listening to the "everlasting gospel."

Tolerance—one of the key words in the end times

"Tolerance" is an interesting word. Its first meaning is the "capacity to endure pain or hardship"; its second meaning is to "show sympathy or indulgence for beliefs or practices differing from or conflicting with one's own."[19]

In recent years, this second meaning has segued into an atmosphere that forbids open discussion of one's personal views;

18. John Leo, "Deaf to good sense," *U.S. News & World Report*, March 25, 2002.

19. Webster's *Ninth New Collegiate Dictionary* (Springfield, MA: Merriam-Webster, Inc., Publishers, 1988).

if those views differ from a *militant minority*, then those views are considered automatically intolerant! Censorship, in a backhanded way, soon trails the skirts of "tolerance." The expression of opposing views, for many, becomes "hate speech;" [20] thus, the expression of different opinions (no matter what the evidence is) reveals intolerance!

All this leads to a society so "tolerant" that a legitimate discussion regarding biblical morality would quickly move beyond free discussion to political incorrectness, to coercion and oppression.[21] In the context of the Great Controversy, such a strategy by Satan is exactly what might be expected in the end time, even in a land that probably has the strictest "free speech" laws in the world![22] How would one have the freedom to discuss historical accuracy and biblical interpretation regarding the Sabbath-Sunday issue in a society that forbids any negative remarks about anybody else's religion?

On February 5, 2006, the Roman Catholic Church released its "Statement on Offending Religious Sentiments," arguing, "Freedom

---

20. Of course, anybody in his or her right mind is against "hate speech" that is abusive, insulting, or intimidating—often leading to violence. Some talk shows are plain shock shows, calculated to vilify and demean others. Words are like bullets and can be turned into bullets. No Christian should defend this kind of "hate speech." No Christian should ostracize gays or lesbians because their belief system contradicts what many feel are a biblical issue. Not only should Christians defend them from "hate speech," they should be defended against "hate discrimination" of any kind. Christians like their Master should value the person, getting beyond a person's clothing or social choices.

21. A student at Boalt Hall, the law school of the University of California-Berkeley, thinks that a long-term trend is developing in that any dissent from the gay agenda constitutes a form of illegitimate speech: "An opinion contrary to the majority opinion at Boalt in favor of gay rights might be treated as the equivalent of racist hate speech." Or open debate on the subject "would be treated as creating a hostile work environment." Cited in John Leo, "Coercion on Campus," *U.S. News & World Report*, May 15, 2000.

22. "The USA, as the least censored society in the world, has held firmly to the First Amendment and to Article 19 of the Universal Declaration of Human Rights, which has meant that attempts to make provision against hate speech have almost all been disallowed by the Supreme Court."—Ursula Owen, "The Speech That Kills," Iain Walker Memorial Lecture, Oxford University, 1999.

of thought and expression cannot imply the right to offend the religious sentiment of believers." The Church said that "Real or verbal intolerance ... is always a serious threat to peace." On the face of it, it seems to promote harmony and peace. But it forces the reader to ask, "What is verbal intolerance?" When the word "sentiment" is used, we are talking about "feelings" and if anyone's feelings are offended, the discussion is a "serious threat to peace."[23] We think of Elijah on Mount Carmel!

But another side of tolerance is the post-modern flood that sweeps away critical thinking: Everyone has the "right" to choose the "truth" that appeals to him or her BECAUSE moral absolutes don't exist! One's personal opinion is as good or as valuable as anyone else's. In that climate, tolerance is expected in religious matters and discussions of moral values, for there is no such thing as "absolute truth"! All this with the perfume of "political correctness." [24] Not only is tolerance expected, it will be enforced by legal means.

Ellen White could not be more relevant:

"The position that it is of no consequence what men believe is one of Satan's most successful deceptions. He knows that the truth, received in the love of it, sanctifies the soul of the receiver; therefore he is constantly seeking to substitute false theories, fables, another gospel."[25]

---

23. *ZENIT*, February 5, 2006, as cited in www.adventcry.org/archive/2005/2-19-2006.

24. The "intellectual's" ideal has been traditionally associated with a commitment to universal truths but history shows that "they" have had difficulty living up to their ideal. Note Heidegger's Nazism in German, Lukács' Fascism in Hungry, and D'Annunzio's Communism in Italy, for starters. But since post-modernism has swept the world, including intellectuals, "the greatest cost of the demise of the intellectuals might be a lack of confidence in those universal principles.'Now,' says McClay, 'even the public senses that there is no bearer of disinterested truth.'"—Jay Tolson, "All Thought Out?" *U. S. News & World Report*, March 11, 2002.

25. *The Great Controversy*, 520. "By the cry, Liberality [or, tolerance, open-mindedness], men are blinded to the devices of their adversary, while he [Satan] is all the time working steadily for the accomplishment of his object. As he succeeds in supplanting the Bible by human speculations, the law of God is set aside, and the churches are under the bondage of sin while they claim to be free."—*The Great Controversy*, 522

George Barna, founder and president of Barna Research Group, has written 31 books, mostly based on research related to church dynamics and spiritual growth. In his book *The Second Coming of the Church*, he reports that "Americans align themselves with values that give them control. ... To the average American, truth is relative to one's values and circumstances. Only one out of four adults—and even fewer teenagers—believe that there is such a thing as absolute moral truth. Human reason and emotion become the paramount determinant to all that is desirable and appropriate."

He continued: "Without absolute truth, there can be no right and wrong. Without right and wrong, there is no such thing as judgment and no such thing as condemnation. If there is no condemnation, there is no need for a Savior."

Barna quoted a 24-year-old: "It's a pretty cool thing because there is no right or wrong when it comes to faith. You believe what you believe, for whatever reasons seem right to you, and nobody can take that away from you. And then, if you change your mind, that's not an admission of failure or being wrong, but just a change of heart or maybe a sign that you've learned or grown. It's not like math. In spiritual matters the playing field is wide open."[26]

For many, truth is what the majority thinks

Talk about *confusion!* For a growing number, truth is whatever the majority thinks it is—or whatever some aggressive minority group might champion regardless of its merits. Allan Bloom noted in 1987 that:

"There is one thing a professor can be absolutely certain: almost every student entering the university believes, or says he believes, that truth is relative. ... The relativity of truth is not a theoretical insight but a moral postulate, the condition of a free society, or so they see it. ... That it is a moral issue for students is revealed by

---

26. *The Second Coming of the Church* (Nashville, TN: Word Publishing, 1998), 61, 62, 75. Newsweek, May 8, 2000, in its cover story, "What Teens Believe," noted: "Rather than seeking absolute truths in doctrine, they cross denominational boundaries. ... In place of strict adherence to doctrine, many teens embrace a spirit of eclecticism and a suspicion of absolute truths."

the character of their response when challenged—a combination of disbelief and indignation. ... The danger they have been taught to fear from absolutism is not error but intolerance. ... The students, of course, cannot defend their opinion. It is something with which they have been indoctrinated. The best they can do is point out all opinions and cultures there are and have been. What right, they ask, do I or anyone else have to say one is better than the others?"[27]

Satan obviously has done his work well! And his pitch for tolerance gathers momentum: "In 2001, more than 29.4 million Americans said they had no religion—more than double the number in 1990—according to the American Religious Identification Survey 2001 (AIRS). People with no religion now account for 14 percent of the nation, up from 8 percent ... in 1990. ... For them, Sundays are just another Saturday."[28]

In a nutshell, "tolerance" and "love" become interchangeable; "diversity" means everyone can express themselves except Christians, especially Christians who are faithful to the teachings of Jesus. Code words such as "sensitivity training" and "multiculturalism" reflect the lowest common denominator on which "diversity" will unite the majority. "Civility" becomes a code word for "nonjudgmentalism."

"Absolutophobia"[29] pejoratively describes those who say that

---

27. Allan Bloom, *The Closing of the American Mind* (New York: Simon & Schuster, Inc., 1988), 25, 26.

28. *USA Today*, Thursday, March 7, 2002. "According to the World Values Survey, conducted by sociologists in 65 nations since 1981, 'We see (a religious attitude) when we ask how often people spend time thinking about the meaning and purpose of life. We see it in people's attitude toward the environment and in the growth of a worldview that sees all life as sacred and invests nature with dignity and sacred quality. ... 'Thou shalt not pollute' is a new commandment that has snuck into the canon, even in public schools where old-fashioned moral instruction is supposedly taboo. The environmental and peace and gender-equality movements are clearly inculcating values without being specifically religious. ... Contrary to the well-known secularization theory that God is dead and will soon drop off the consciousness map, the USA is a holdout. Spirituality is actually growing in USA."—*USA Today*, March 7, 2002.

29. John Leo, "A no-fault Holocaust," *U.S. News & World Report*, July 21, 1997.

some behavior or ideas are just plain wrong. Campuses of America are awash with teachers and students who deny the existence of objective truth: All they can discuss is differences in perspective.

Thus, in many pulpits, as well as in academic centers, the word "judgment" and "judgmental" are suddenly condemned. After all, who has a right to "judge" anyone if everyone has a right to his or her own opinion! For many modern pulpits, "grace" trumps "judgment"—as if those two words are antithetical!

William J. Bennett wrote, "It is, therefore, past time for what novelist Tom Wolfe has called the 'great relearning.' We have engaged in a frivolous dalliance with dangerous theories— relativism, historicism, and values clarification. Now, when faced with evil on such a grand scale [September 11, 2001], we should see these theories for what they are: empty. We must begin to have the courage of our convictions, to believe that some actions are good and some evil and to act on those beliefs to prevent evil."[30]

This most brief overview of this remarkable and rapid drift from moral absolutes to a spirituality that is measured by feeling and opinion is chiefly due to dismay with the doctrinal confusion that abounds in Christian churches generally.

Doctrinal Confusion

But the confusion reaches beyond Christianity when leading "conservative" rabbis representing the majority of Jews in the United States are telling their congregations that "the story of Noah was probably borrowed from the Mesopotamian epic Gilgamesh," "that the way the Bible describes the Exodus is not the way it happened, if it happened at all," that archeologists digging in the Sinai have "found no trace of the tribes of Israel—not one shard of pottery," "that the 'tales' of Genesis ... were a mix of myth legend, distant memory and search for origins, bound together by the strands of a central theological concept." Liberal Protestants

---

30. "Count one blessing out of 9-11 tragedy: moral clarity," *Houston Chronicle*, October 7, 2001.

have been talking like that for more than a century—but now "conservative" Jewish leaders?[31]

Ellen White foresaw this religious crisis and nailed its cause:

"The vague and fanciful interpretations of Scripture, and the many conflicting theories concerning religious faith, that are found in the Christian world, are the work of our great adversary, to confuse minds so that they shall not discern the truth. And the discord and division which exist among the churches of Christendom are in a great measure due to the prevailing custom of wresting the Scriptures to support a favorite theory."[32]

After years of looking at church squabbles over petty doctrinal arguments, after observing that loyal church goers are not much better people than non-goers, after hearing the limited gospel preached every weekend, whether in pulpits, on TV or radio, where the most they hear is a gospel of free forgiveness but not the gospel that includes responsibility and divine power to transform the life—is it any wonder that restless youth, as well as their jaded parents, are voting with their feet?[33]

---

31. Michael Massing, "As Rabbis Face Facts, Bible Tales Are Wilting," www. nytimes.com. 2000/03/09.

32. *The Great Controversy*, 520.

33. Barna, op. cit. After his extended research, Barna concedes that "we [Christians] think and behave no differently from anyone else." Then, on page 6, he proceeded to give examples of similarities of behavior between Christians and non-Christians: Have been divorced (among those who have been married)—Christians: 27%; non-Christians, 23%. Gave money to a homeless person or poor person in past year—Christians: 24%; non-Christians: 34%. Took drugs or medication prescribed by physician in past year—Christians: 7%; non-Christians: 8%. Watched an X-rated movie in the past 3 months—Christians: 9%; non-Christians: 16%; Donated any money to a nonprofit organization in past month—Christians: 47%; non-Christians: 48%. Bought a lottery ticket in the past week—Christians: 23%; non-Christians: 27%. Feel completely or very successful in life—Christians: 58%; non-Christians: 49%. It is impossible to get ahead because of your financial debt—Christians: 33%; non-Christians: 39%. You are still trying to figure out the purpose of your life—Christians: 36%; non-Christians: 47%. Satisfied with your life these days—Christians: 69%; non-Christians: 68%. Your personal financial situation is getting better—Christians: 27%; non-Christians: 28%.

On October 21, 2003, George Barna announced his update of "Americans Describe Their Views About Life After Death." After reporting divergent views, Barna pointed out that "Americans' willingness to embrace beliefs that are logically contradictory and their preference for blending different faith views together create unorthodox religious viewpoints. ... Millions of Americans have redefined grace to mean that God is so eager to save people from Hell that He will change His nature and universal principles for their individual benefit. It is astounding how many people develop their faith according to their feelings or cultural assumptions rather than biblical teachings."[34]

Control and Coercion

Where is all this pretense, scapegoating, and confusion heading? Where it always ends up—in coercion, the use of power to control or destroy the hated minority. Satan, working through world authorities, will grant "power ... and cause as many as would not worship the image of the beast to be killed" (Revelation 13:15). In crisis, politically correct legislation will appear so timely and necessary that all offenders should be killed!

But all is not bleak! The Great Controversy between God and Satan will not go on forever! Reckoning day is just ahead! Ideas and decisions surely have consequences, and it comes down to freedom and coercion. The Bible previews that moment when time is running out for Planet Earth.

The issue comes down to when God's loyalists are sealed and those who reject God's messages receive the Mark of the Beast and worship its image. Two groups are finally and clearly distinguished.

God's loyalists reflect the character of Jesus; Satan's loyalists reflect his character. The last time we saw this clearly distinguished was at the Cross! Satan did his best to beat Jesus down, physically and emotionally—awful pressure. And he will do his best to beat down our Lord's faithful, in every way possible, when he has the

---

34. www.barna.org/cgi-bin//PagePressRelease.asp? (October 24, 2003).

greater majority of all worldly inhabitants primed to destroy those stubborn Sabbath-keepers.

Satan's hate is never calm. Ultimate selfishness lashes out unrestrained. And that is exactly what we see in the biblical overview of the seven last plagues—cartoon-like pictures of unrestrained evil, selfishness, and rage. The wicked have been sheltered for years from the full venom of the Dragon (Satan) by the grace of God reaching for their hearts. But after probation has closed, after each person has chosen either to worship the God of the Fourth Commandment or the false gods represented by Babylon, the wicked, by their own choice, no longer are protected from evil forces in the universe.[35]

As the plagues begin to fall, those who are worshiping the image of the beast (Revelation 13:15) have further "reason" to hate God's loyalists. They have been "enraged" with the power that attended the "loud cry" and "their anger is kindled against all who have received the message." And now "those who honor the law of God have been accused of bringing judgments upon the world and they will be regarded as the cause of the fearful convulsions of nature and the strife and bloodshed among men that are filling the earth with woe."[36] They now blame all these terrible plagues on God's faithful as if they are responsible for what seems, to them, to be the anger of God!

This malignant rage aimed at those who fearlessly stand for freedom in a very troubled, angry world soon results in not a stiffer Sunday law, but a new way to eliminate the Sabbath-keepers in their "semblance of zeal for God."[37] That new "way," unknown to

---

35. "Unsheltered by divine grace, they have no protection from the wicked one. Satan will then plunge the inhabitants of the earth into one great, final trouble. As the angels of God cease to hold in check the fierce winds of human passion, all the elements of strife will be let loose. The whole world will be involved in ruin more terrible than that which came upon Jerusalem of old. ... The same destructive power exercised by holy angels when God commands, will be exercised by evil angels when He permits. There are forces now ready, and only waiting the divine permission, to spread desolation everywhere. —*The Great Controversy*, 614.

36. Ibid., 614, 615.

37. Ibid., 615.

the United States and so contrary to its historical principles, will be a Sabbath "decree," denouncing Sabbath-keepers "as deserving of the severest punishment, and giving the people [those worshipping the beast and its image] liberty, after a certain time, to put them to death."[38]

The entire universe will see the ultimate hatred of ultimate evil once more. When the fiendish rage of Satan is focused on God's loyalists in this last hour of the end times, the universe will see again what happened at the cross—evil will again has its way, but only for a little while.

Summary

Satan has practiced his strategy for control of God's world of intelligent beings ever since his revolt in heaven. His tactics are always the same—pretense, scapegoating, confusion, and finally control through coercion.

God's loyalists will face up to these satanic weapons as Jesus did. They will keep fresh in their minds the truth about God. They will not be distracted by evil's attempts to blame others for the "mess" evil is causing. They will keep their minds on core truths of the gospel so that ordinary ways of using language are not confused with the subtlety of "progressive" thinking. They will foresee how evil attempts to control and coerce, taking courage in the warmth of others who also see the danger.

It has never been this late before! We all are living in the time when Satan's ferocity against God and His loyalists overflows all previous assaults. Let us keep our minds alert and our vision focused on the key elements of the Great Controversy that will soon end. The payoff is out of this world!

---

38. Ibid., 615.

> Theme: Jesus will return when the gospel
> in its fullness is "preached in all the world"
> (Matthew 24:14).

♦ CHAPTER EIGHT ♦

Catching the Steady Trend of Events

*I*t has never been this late before!

We have been warned that "the final movements will be rapid ones,"[1] that "perplexities ... scarcely dreamed of are before us,"[2] that "events of the future ... will soon come upon [us] with blinding force,"[3] that "a storm is coming, relentless in its fury,"[4] that "no one [should] feel that he is secure from the danger of being surprised,"[5] that we should be preparing for what is about "to break upon the world as an overwhelming surprise,"[6] and that we should be able to "catch the steady tread of the events."[7]

---

1. *Testimonies*, vol. 9, 11.

2. Ibid. 43.

3. *Manuscript Releases*, vol. 4, 74.

4. *Testimonies*, vol. 8, 315.

5. *Last-Day Events*, 16.

6. *Testimonies*, vol. 8, 28.

7. *Testimonies*, vol. 7, 14.

159

In view of what you have read in this book, is it possible that some will still say, "I never saw it coming!" Or "Why didn't someone tell us?"

But what I must insist is this: Even though we have drilled in on seven key areas that will certainly converge on the last generation, no one knows precisely how all or anyone of these areas, such as natural disasters, economic distress, papal influence, Sunday laws, psychic phenomena, etc., will exactly happen in specific detail.

We have only painted the picture of the last days as clearly as we now have information in any of these areas. I assure you, I know that I will be profoundly "surprised" at how the "rapid movements" will develop with "blinding force." But I can say without ambiguity that the coming "storm" that each of the areas highlighted in this book accentuate will truly be "relentless in its fury." And together, the combined effect will catch us all with "overwhelming surprise." All of us! But the better we are prepared, the easier it will be to balance ourselves when we are surprised!

One of the clearest predictions Jesus made regarding the last generation is found in Matthew 24:14—"And this gospel of the kingdom will be preached in all the world as a witness to all the nations, and then the end will come."

We do not need a college degree to understand what our Lord is saying. Millions of Christians are focused on getting their message out to "all the world." I commend the energy and personal sacrifice that hundreds of thousands are devoting to their particular denomination's mission programs. Those who resent their presence are killing many thousands of them annually. Since 1907 when the slogan was first coined by a Protestant mission board, many denominations have focused on taking the "gospel to all the world in this generation."

"This" Gospel

On closer examination to our Lord's prediction, we note that He said "*this* gospel." Even in the first 50 years after He returned to heaven, Paul said that he had to contend with "a *different* gospel." In the 2,000 years since, any teenager can see that there are many gospels in the world, so many in direct contradictions to each other. What shall we make of all this?

▶ We must get back to what Jesus considered the "good news" to be. Remember, He was talking to His disciples before His crucifixion! Obviously, there was something about the gospel that must go to all the world before He returns that He had been teaching His disciples up to that moment.

▶ We must work ourselves through the many "different" gospels in the world today in order to find "this gospel" that must go to "all the world." Something more than repeating the name of Jesus and the fact that He was crucified would be needed.

▶ We must join together the grace of pardon and the grace of power.

▶ We must ever keep in view that the purpose of the gospel is not only forgiveness, but also restoration of everything spoiled by sin.

▶ We must give special attention to the "everlasting gospel" that John the Revelator said would be timely and urgent in the end times: "Then I saw another angel flying in the midst of heaven, having the everlasting gospel to preach to those who dwell on the earth—to every nation, tribe, tongue, and people" (14:6).

▶ We must recognize that there is something very important about the "everlasting gospel" that has been forgotten or corrupted—that must be recovered in the last days.

▶ The recovered "everlasting gospel" is not the limited gospel that so many good and dedicated Christians have been proclaiming.

▶ The "everlasting gospel" is the complete gospel that is being recovered by those who are "saying with a loud voice, 'Fear God and give glory to Him, for the hour of His judgment has come" (14:7).

▶ Those proclaiming worldwide this "everlasting gospel" are identified in verse 12: "Here is the patience [Greek: endurance] of the saints, here are those who keep the commandments of God and the faith of Jesus."

World Statistics

As far as I have been able to determine, the Seventh-day Adventist Church is now in 204 of the 233 nations recognized by the United Nations.[8] That means at this time, Adventists do not have any identifiable presence in 26 countries, such as Yemen, United Arab Emirates, Saudi Arabia, Tunisia, Somali, North Korea, Bhutan, and Brunei.

Looking at it another way, the estimated population of the world, as of June 2004, was 6,395,892,000. The estimated population of the world in which Adventists are established is 6,291,872,394. The estimated population of the countries where Adventists do not have an identifiable presence is 104,019,605.

When we look at the world field, 20 percent of Adventists are in South America; 16 percent in East Central Africa; 14 percent in InterAmerica; 17 percent in South Africa/Indian Ocean; twelve percent in Southern Asia; compared to three and one half percent in North America, and 26/100th of one percent in Tran European Division (with other divisions making up the rest). Thirty-five percent of world Adventists live in Latin America and 35 percent are in African divisions.

The ratio of Adventists to total population is interesting: Adventists are 1 in 459 in the world field. In Peru, 1 in 41; in the Philippines, 1 in 111; in Brazil, 1 in135; in the United States, 1 in 309; in India, 1 in 1,185.

In the year 2004 (the last year for full statistics), Seventh-day Adventist membership increased 1,452 *each day.* On an average day, six new churches were established and 2,933 people were baptized.

What does all this mean? It means much work remains to be · done. Is it an impossible task? Absolutely not! What kind of burden rested on the disciples after Jesus returned to heaven—that surely *looked* like the impossible!

---

8. Seventh-day Adventist 142nd Annual Statistical Report, 2004. http://ast. gc.adventist.org

Seemed Impossible

Let's enjoy a little perspective. I admit that in 1950, it seemed impossible unless the Lord wrote the gospel on the clouds by day and traced it with laser beams on the sky by night. Today, at the beginning of the 21st century, the world is almost saturated with many sources of communication that we didn't even dream of in 1950.

Think of the internet—no country's passport, visa, border patrol, etc., can forbid it. One of the biggest surprises I found in my travels in the Orient and in the 10-40 window was the forest of television antennae I saw—over some of the most dilapidated shanties. Add the internet and TV to FM radio and shortwave radio—one can blanket the world without fear of border patrols!

In many, if not most, of the 26 countries where Adventists have no identifiable presence, these modern communication marvels are present. Many of our Adventist media programs, such as Amazing Facts, It is Written, Voice of Prophecy, The Quiet Hour, and others are blanketing most of these countries even as we write. Written requests for Bible school lessons require constant increasing of staff and space. These Adventist outreaches are even carrying on live internet conversations with people who wouldn't dare attend a public meeting.

Bottom line: The Adventist challenge is not *how* we are to reach honest seekers for truth. The highest challenge is *what* kind of gospel are they hearing! Above all other items on the Adventist agenda should be a constant review of what kind of a gospel we are proclaiming. How different is the Adventist gospel from our Roman Catholic friends who devote much energy and funds in their missionary outreach? We say, much in everyway!

What about our Baptist friends or Pentecostal friends? They too have an enormous missionary program that in many countries are far more advanced than we are. How different is the Adventist gospel compared to Baptists and Pentecostals?

What about the worldwide expansion of mega-churches, such as Rick Warren's Saddleback Church or Bill Hybel's Willow Creek? How different is the Adventist gospel? In what respects?

The only way Christ's prophecy will be fulfilled is when Adventists, embracing the responsibility of proclaiming the "everlasting gospel," truly do just that!

Good Witnesses

But there is another aspect of Matthew 24:14 that we must constantly remember: only good "witnesses" can tell the truth about the gospel. This connection between God's commission to the church—that the Christian's reflection of His character and principles would be His "witness" to the world, and that the return of Jesus depends on when this "witness" has been faithfully done— is neatly summarized in these words:

> "It is the darkness of misapprehension of God that is enshrouding the world. Men are losing their knowledge of His character. It has been misunderstood and misinterpreted. At this time a message from God is to be proclaimed, a message illuminating in its influence and saving in its power. His character is to be made known. Into the darkness of the world is to be shed the light of His glory, the light of His goodness, mercy, and truth. ... Those who wait for the Bridegroom's coming are to say to the people, 'Behold your God.' The last rays of merciful light, the last message of mercy to be given to the world, is a revelation of His character of love. The children of God are to manifest His glory. In their own life and character they are to reveal what the grace of God has done for them. The light of the Sun of Righteousness is to shine forth in good works—in words of truth and deeds of holiness."[9]

This is an amazing statement. Frankly, very unambiguous! It simply amplifies our Lord's prediction: "This gospel of the kingdom will be preached in all the world as a *witness* to all the nations, and then shall the end come" (Matthew 24:14).

Witnesses in any court must not repeat hearsay! They can speak only of what they personally know. God's faithful in the end times will be personal witnesses to what the gospel has done

---

9. *Christ's Object Lessons*, 415, 416.

for them and what it will surely do for all those who also "come and see."

Could it be said any clearer?

"All who receive Christ as a personal Saviour are to demonstrate the truth of the gospel and its saving power upon the life. God makes no requirement without making provision for its fulfillment. Through the grace of Christ we may accomplish everything that God requires. All the riches of heaven are to be revealed through God's people. 'Herein is My Father glorified,' Christ says, 'that ye bear much fruit; so shall ye be My disciples. John 15:8."[10]

God waits for His professed people to step up to their responsibilities. He restrains Satan from having his last hurrah in attempting to capture the world, once and for all. We call that awful time the "seven last plagues."

When Jesus Returns

If anyone asks, "When will Jesus return?" turn to Revelation 7 and say, "When God finds enough people whom He can stamp with His seal of approval!"

In other words, God is holding back the satanic fury of the seven last plagues. Why? He is waiting for His people to catch on as to the purpose of the gospel and to act accordingly. He is waiting for people on whom He can write His signature as His forever endorsement, people He can finally use in completing the gospel commission of Matthew 24:14. These will be people who have our "Father's name written on their foreheads ... and in their mouth was found no guile for they are without fault before the throne of God" (14:1, 5). But there is more: these are last-day witnesses to the power and purpose of the gospel; God Himself will testify to

---

10. Ibid., 301. "The world today is in crying need of a revelation of Christ Jesus in the person of His saints. God desires that His people shall stand before the world a holy people. Why?—because there is a world to be saved by the light of gospel truth; and as the message of truth that is to call men out of darkness into God's marvelous light is given by the church, the lives of its members, sanctified by the Spirit of truth, are to bear witness to the verity of the messages proclaimed" *Testimonies to Ministers,* 458.

166 NEVER BEEN THIS LATE BEFORE

their faithfulness and "they shall see His face, and His name shall be on their foreheads (22:4).

What a privilege, what a responsibility, what a future!

In 1857, two editorials appeared in *Harper's Weekly*, a widely read periodical"—

"It is a gloomy moment in history. Not for many years—not in the lifetime of most men who read this paper—has there been so much grave and deep apprehension; never has the future seemed so incalculable as at this time. In our own country there is a universal commercial prostration and panic and thousands of our poorest fellow-citizens are burned out against the approaching winter without employment, and without the prospects of it. In France the political caldron seethes and bubbles with uncertainty; Russia hangs as usual, like a cloud dark and silent upon the horizon of Europe; while all the energies, resources and influences of the British Empire are sorely tried, and are yet to be tried more sorely. ...

"It is a solemn moment, and no man can feel an indifference— which happily, no man pretends to feel—in the issue of events. Of our own troubles no man can see the end. They are fortunately, as yet mainly commercial, and if we are only to lose money, and by painful poverty to be taught wisdom—the wisdom of honor, of faith, of sympathy, and of charity—no man need seriously to despair. And yet the very haste to be rich, which is the occasion of this wide-spread calamity, has also tended to destroy the moral forces with which we are to resist and subdue the calamity." [October 10, 1857].

"The sun is setting—the air is chill—health is failing; there are no stars—there is only universal ignorance, regret, grief, and despair. It is easy enough to say that we are in the woods, it is easy to see that we are—for a time at least—lost; it is not difficult to know that we came in of our own accord." [October 17, 1857].

With minor editing, these words could easily be mirrored in many magazines and newspapers throughout the world—even today. Living in 1857 with its financial troubles was tough, but they had no idea of the enormous convergences of last-day troubles we have been discussing. The day is fast coming when we all will be writing similar words for ourselves but with far more reason—"the sun is setting, the air is chill."

I found Pope Benedict XVI's message to the world on Good Friday, April 14, 2006 strangely echoing our *Harper's Weekly* editor:

"Lord, we have lost our sense of sin. Today a slick campaign of propaganda is spreading an inane apologia of evil, a senseless cult of Satan, a mindless desire for transgression, a dishonest and frivolous freedom, exalting impulsiveness, immorality and selfishness as if they were new heights of sophistication. ...

"Lord Jesus, our affluence is making us less human, our entertainment has become a drug, a source of alienation, and our society's incessant, tedious message is an invitation to die of selfishness."

Evil Pervasive

I think of those ghastly shrieks of the al Qaeda terrorist as he steered United Airlines Flight 93 on September 11, 2001, into southwestern Pennsylvania: "Allah Akbar! Allah is the greatest!" How evil can evil get? We haven't seen anything yet!

For those who have found their hope, courage, and joy in the "everlasting gospel," the darkening twilight of these last days only makes the return of their Lord that much nearer! Their trust and faith is not in themselves but in their Lord who showed them how to live and how to die.

Ted Turner's Sign-Off Tape

Not everyone has this truth and faith. Ted Turner is best known for founding TBS and CNN and his $1 billion pledge to the United Nations. He also is America's largest private landowner, owning more than two million acres (greater than Delaware and Rhode Island combined), including 14 ranches in six states. One of his interesting quotes is: "I'd rather go to hell. Heaven has got to be boring."

But with all his wealth and prestige, he is known for his doom and gloom. When he launched CNN in 1980, he said: "We gonna go on air June 1, and we gonna stay on until the end of the world. When that time comes, we'll cover it, play 'Nearer, My God, to Thee' over footage of a waving American flag." Turner ordered the tape locked away until it was determined that the world was about to end.

One source said, "It was like a sign-off tape that you often see in the middle of the night—but to Ted, was a sign-off forever."

I remember a speaking appointment in Corpus Christi, Texas, a few years ago. During some free time, my wife and I visited the *USS Lexington*, anchored in the harbor. It is the fifth ship in U.S. history to have that brave name. The fourth was lost in the Battle of the Coral Sea (May 1942) after a brilliant and heroic effort that stopped the advance of the Japanese toward Australia. As soon as this news hit America, the next aircraft carrier being built was named the *Lexington*, which also soon saw gallant action in the Pacific.

"This is the captain speaking"

On December 4, 1943, a Japanese bomber disabled this new *Lexington* on a moonlit night off Tarawa. The skipper, Captain Felix Stump, went to the ship speaker system so that all aboard could hear him: "This is the captain speaking. We have taken a torpedo hit in our stern and the rudder seems badly damaged. *Each man must do his job calmly and efficiently. Don't worry. That's my job. I got you here and I'll get you out and home."* Marvelous story of how they limped home!

But there's more to the story. More than 95 percent of those on board had never been in the open sea before. They were not seasoned sailors and pilots. Citizen sailors and pilots they were. Recently assembled, trained, but unsure of themselves. On that moonlit night, they were an easy target, but the captain kept maneuvering the ship to face into the moonlight so that the *Lexington* would not give the bomber or submarine a broadside silhouette. All the time changing his speed and direction.

On the way back to Pearl Harbor with that disabled rudder, the Admiral of the fleet radioed to Captain Stump, "That was wonderful seamanship, Captain." The Captain replied, "*Thank you, sir, my crew was magnificent!*"

Those words swept through the crew: They were "magnificent" in the eyes of their captain! The sailors wrote home about their captain. When they limped back to Pearl, they didn't need the serenade of the Navy Band to make them feel like they were heroes. They had already heard the commendation of their captain. Knowing their captain for what he was kept them unafraid, kept them doing their duty. They could trust their captain, because he got them there and he would get them home.

One of these days, a wonderful group of people will, in a way, limp into the Harbor after the worst time of trouble ever to hit people on this earth. And they will hear their Captain say: "Well done, good and faithful servants. ... Enter into the joy of your lord" (Matthew 25:21).

And then He will turn to the unfallen worlds, to the unfallen angels, and wave His hand over the veterans from earth, and say, "My crew was magnificent!"

Here were the people upon whom God risked His integrity and government. In a very special way, the rest of the universe that had been watching Laboratory Earth will stand and salute these veterans of a very costly war! And then turn to their Captain of the universe and fall on their knees in a sob that will echo from galaxy to galaxy—a sob of relief and gratitude and love! The risk was worth it!

It has never been this late before!